# Endorsement for *Bullet, Paper, Rock*

*Bullet, Paper, Rock* is a kind of wonder-room of glimpses of childhood and youth in Lebanon, of family entanglements, migration, war and, above all, language, the trilingual man's love affair with language. The writer's English is startling in its serenity and precision against a seething background of loss and calamity, at once personal and universal. Abbas El-Zein speaks about the things that matter most to everyone. His voice is not one you will easily forget.

**Robert Dessaix**

# Bullet, Paper, Rock

**Abbas El-Zein**

Abbas El-Zein has written two acclaimed works of fiction – a novel, *Tell the Running Water* and a collection of short stories, *The Secret Maker of the World* – as well as an award-winning memoir, *Leave to Remain*. Abbas has published essays and short stories about war, identity and displacement for *HEAT Magazine, The New York Times, The Guardian, The Age, Meanjin, Overland* and *Tank Magazine*. He is professor of environmental engineering at the University of Sydney.

Abbas El-Zein

# Bullet, Paper, Rock

A Memoir of Words and Wars

UPSWELL

First published in Australia in 2024
Revised and reprinted in 2025
by Upswell Publishing
Perth, Western Australia
upswellpublishing.com

Upswell operates in the city of Perth, on ancient country of the Whadjuk people of the Noongar nation who remain the spiritual and cultural custodians of this beautiful land. We acknowledge their continuing connection to country and express gratitude to elders past and present for their strength and creativity…Always was, always will be, Aboriginal land.

ISBN: 978-0-645-87453-2

A catalogue record for this book is available from the National Library of Australia

Cover design by Chil3, Fremantle
Typeset in Foundry Origin by Lasertype
Printed by Lightning Source

I wonder at a love
 that flaunts its glory
among the garden
 flowers, she said
Don't, I said
 You're seeing yourself
in the mirror
 of humankind

**Muhyiddeen Ibn Arabi**, translated by Michael Sells


Every city street is a stage – every stage, a staging of desire.

**Robin Robertson**, *The Long Take*

Several names in this memoir have been changed.

# Contents

A foray is an incursion into unyielding territory or the temporary conquest of a hostile stretch of land. The word comes from the French *forager*, to search for food in nature. A foray is probing and uncertain, sometimes a prelude to something bigger.

There is, to my mind, such a thing as a literary foray. Like other kinds of essays, a foray can be nourishing and exploratory. It may draw on introspective insights and, like other essays, may 'digress' and revel in 'luck and play', just as soldiers, outlaws and fortune seekers do.

But a foray cannot afford to indulge in self-reflection for too long, because what preoccupies it most is the world and its manifold realities. It is less meandering, perhaps – has a stronger sense of purpose – than other kinds of essays. There is an anxious urgency to it: it expects difficulty, hostility, even possible defeat and symbolic death. What it desires, unlike most essays, are a lightning victory, some well-earned spoils and, above all, a homecoming.

# ONE:
# CHILDHOOD

# Ever After

I must have been eight or nine when, on a summer day in the early 1970s, on our way back to Beirut from a visit to our ancestral village of Jibsheet in the south of Lebanon, my family stopped in the coastal city of Saida for a dip in the Mediterranean.

I had been taught how to swim in the Lebanese, carefree sort of way that consists of dropping the child in the water and watching them drown a little, lifting them out and dropping them again, until they have learnt how to float – not exactly a recipe for producing Olympic swimmers but one that seems to work, nonetheless.

We were a rowdy family – seven of us on that day: my parents, three older sisters, infant brother and me – and there was safety in numbers and loving affection. So much so, it took me a while to understand that I was being pulled by a rip into the open sea and that my feeble arms were no match for it. I was a slight child and, in our household, brain rated higher than brawn, a case perhaps of making a virtue out of necessity.

Pride must have played a part in delaying the moment at which to call for help and, when that moment came, I had drifted too far to be heard. I had spent enough time poring over our illustrated atlas to know my travel options.

The nearest land to the west was Cyprus, a country that, although conceivably close, was as foreign as they came, since people there spoke Cypriot, a Greek dialect, rather than Arabic. Besides, I liked clarity on maps and the Cypriots couldn't seem to make up their minds whether they were Greek or Turkish. This was admittedly rich, coming from a Lebanese, but I would only come to realise this much later in life.

I spoke French, so Monaco, the easternmost point on the *Hexagone*, was an option in theory but I would have had to overcome the not-inconsiderable difficulty of the Italian boot sticking out into the sea and blocking my way. Besides, even in my most fantasy-prone moments, I knew that Italy, let alone France, was way too far. I could try heading north, up the Syrian coast, past the port city of Laathiqiyya, all the way to Istanbul – which I would ultimately reach because of the way the Turkish landmass turned to the left all of a sudden, as if it had had a change of heart halfway through geological genesis. But then there was the language barrier again. Or I could try aiming south and, provided I stayed clear of Israeli gunboats and the now European-settled Palestinian coast, might reach Cairo or even the Mersa Matrouh resort town, further west – Egyptian landmarks on which I was a self-proclaimed expert through my avid reading of the 'Five Adventurers' series of books.

Besides, if I were to reach the Egyptian coast, I could draw on a solid store of expressions I had gleaned from the Egyptian movies that my mother liked to watch. *Bahibbik ya Fatma, ana mush adra ya Mahmoud* or, a little more dramatically, *inte tali', tali', tali'* – 'I hereby divorce thee'. I could no doubt talk my way to the airport and catch a plane back to Beirut, perhaps even in time for dinner.

But if these thoughts had crossed my mind, providing a brief escape from my predicament, the ache in my puny biceps would have brought me back to reality. I was flailing, beating away at the water to stay afloat, but still facing the shore, hoping someone in my family would see me. My voice was already weak from yelling, and I was terrified by the invisible rip dragging me away from everything I had ever known.

And then, just as panic had taken hold, I felt myself being lifted into the air and thrust towards the shore, as if on some small, magical hovercraft. It took me a few moments to understand that my silent saviour was a man who had been swimming out in the sea, saw me struggling and came to my rescue from behind, the V shape of one hand holding me by the underarm, its grip squeezing my tiny ribcage, giving me a wonderful tug to the heart. A few minutes later, he delivered me to my mother's lap, exchanged a few words with my father, graciously acknowledged the multiple thank-yous of my shocked parents, then dived back into the sea.

I never saw my saviour again and do not recall his face, except for the sketchiest of outlines. But I *believed* in him, ever after, as I watched him disappear into the sea, my gratitude as great as my earlier terror. I was so awestruck, so exhausted, so speechless with relief that, had he suddenly turned around and said that he was a merman living in the deep ocean and had shot up to the surface when he heard my call for help – some kind of Abdallah of the Sea, straight from a Thousand and One Nights tale; or that he was one of those djinns, mentioned in the Quran, that God had sent in disguise to rescue me; or even that he was an extraordinary human – a knight-in-swimsuit – who just happened to be standing idly on a beach in Limassol, two hundred kilometres away, noticed my struggles and swam all the way to pull me out of the water, in a mountain-coming-to-Mohammad sort of way, I would not have doubted his word for one moment.

# The Kindergarten Years

I have no memory of this event but, once my mother mentions it to me in passing as an adult, I start seeing it with unwelcome clarity.

I am led by my father out of our apartment, into the lift, through the gate, down the narrow street, under an overcast sky, watched over by buildings on both sides. We are crossing the fifty metres or so towards the street junction where the school bus picks up kids. I am sobbing and, when I see the bus waiting, I break into hysterical screams, drag my feet, and try to turn around and run the other way but fail to free my hand from my father's grip. I know my mother can hear me, up on the third floor, perhaps even see me if she's on the balcony. Unlike in Isaac's tale, there is no last-moment reprieve for me – God is not testing anyone's faith on this occasion. Only a dumb-mute giant of a building, my father's unyielding hand and this brick of an ache crushing my ribcage. Every morning, Sisyphus-like. Until, one day, the memory fades out of my consciousness and settles into my bones: until, that is, I become the forgetting of it.

# Manaal

*Manaal* is a formal Arabic word which doubles up as a female first name. The word is most encountered in the expression *naalat manaalaha*, literally 'she earned what she wanted', but more generally 'she fulfilled her wish' (or *naala manaalahu* for a male subject).

But *manaal* is not the same as *raghba* (desire), *mashee'a* or *umnia* (wish) or *haaja* (need). It comes from the root word *naala*, for earned or acquired. That is, *manaal* refers to desire *but only if it's been satisfied*. Although it can be used in a negative sentence – *she has not fulfilled her wish* – it retains its prevalent sense of desire achieved.

The English word 'earnings', though formally similar because it comes from 'earn' and indicates something already in one's possession, is a wholly inadequate translation: the Arabic *manaal* does not carry the slightest pecuniary connotation. *Manaal*'s closest synonyms in Arabic are *maraad* and *mubtagha*, both of which mean 'that which one wants' but without any implication that the desiring subject has acquired it. Unlike *manaal*.

Someone, somewhere, once had the brilliant insight that a desire fulfilled is of a separate kind, of a different nature, to its more generic counterparts, and deserves an exquisite little word of its own.

# I Dream of Jeannie

One of the picture books of *Alf Layla wa Layla*, the Thousand and One Nights, that I read when I was a child had a drawing of Shahrazaad wearing light-blue garments, a veil hanging from the bridge of her nose, a diaphanous scarf covering her hair and the back of her neck, a long-sleeved midriff top leaving her cleavage uncovered and a pair of 'harem' pants gathered at the ankles. The closest to this image I remember seeing elsewhere – either before or after my first encounter with this picture book, I am not sure – was in the American sitcom *I Dream of Jeannie*, in which the very blond Barbara Eden plays a charming djinn who falls in love with an astronaut played by Larry Hagman, in a very American suburban setting.

In my picture book, Shahrazaad was sitting on a carpeted floor with her legs bent to one side, her back straight, beside the front leg of a divan where King Shahrayaar was lying. Shahrayaar had a rounded face with a curly beard, an embroidered turban worn slightly askew, and a shock of hair falling over his broad forehead. He was staring at Shahrazaad with fascination: the expression could have been a smile or a grimace. The two faces were uncomfortably close, their gazes locked, while a bunch of grapes dangled, neglected, from Shahrayaar's hand. The picture left me in no doubt as to which of the two wielded more power. But

A scene from sitcom *I Dream of Jeannie*.

Shahrayaar's power appeared to have been temporarily suspended by something Shahrazaad had done.

Turning the page and reading the frame tale of *Alf Layla*, I understood what the picture meant: every night, Shahrazaad, a shrewd storyteller, entertained the king with a new story that she left unresolved until the next day. This she did in order to distract the king, seduce him and ultimately convince him to spare her, for he'd intended to kill her. Shahrayaar and his brother Shahzamaan had been stung by the unfaithfulness of their wives, and the king had since been in the habit of deflowering and killing the virgins that his vizier brought to him.

*Alf Layla* was a book of fairy tales, with a female hero, to sit alongside Cinderella, Sleeping Beauty, Leila and the Wolf, and Le Petit Poucet. It was full of delightful stories such as Aladdin and the Magic Lamp, and Ali Baba and the Forty Thieves.

Or so I thought. In truth, while my abridged and highly sanitised book offered itself as fairy tales for children, I would find out later that this was far from an apt description of *Alf Layla*. As it happened, Shahrazaad was having sex with the king every night before sharing her stories; her sister Duniazaad was there with them all along, 'under the bed' according to one version of the story, not quite a ménage à trois but almost; and the often violent and sometimes sexually explicit stories told by Shahrazaad were not for the faint-hearted and certainly not intended for children. Watching Jeannie again as an adult, there is no doubting the sexual intent of the sitcom too. From the first episode of the first season, seduction, adultery and bare female skin figure prominently, as well as, inevitably, that form of American narcissism which has foreign women falling over themselves for the white male hero (Jeannie routinely calls her man 'master').

I suspect that even as a seven- or eight-year-old I must have reacted sexually to Jeannie without knowing it. After all, it was around that time, or perhaps not long after, that I had my first erection, triggered by an Arabic-language Batman comic, one in which the main villain was Batwoman, whose gleaming leather attire, curvaceous form and exaggeratedly almond-shaped eyes had awoken something perplexingly pleasurable in me.

# Lexicon of Love

Arabic speakers are spoilt for choice when it comes to expressions of love. At least twenty-five Arabic words for different shades of love, affection and love-induced states of mind are in common usage, by my count. The actual number is said to be somewhere between fifty and one hundred, if formal Arabic words, less encountered in day-to-day speech, are included.

*hub, hawaa, gharaam, walaa, hanaan, shaghaf, kalaf, shawq, walah, tatayyum, haneen* ...

No two words have the same meaning, and the vocabulary maps out a range of emotions, moods and relationships with the beloved, while conveying myriad kinds of love – sensual, carnal or chaste, profane or divine, joyful or melancholy.

From love as tenderness (*atf* or *sababa*), forlornness (*wajd*) or feelings of warmth towards someone (*wod*), through chaste (*eeffa*), eternal (*rasseess*) or unrequited (*lajaa*) love, to adulation (*oshq*), infatuation (*wallah*) and passionate love (*hiaam*). Love that leaves us burning is *huraaq* and love that stings is *lathgh*. There is suppressed love (*kamad*), love as joy and enjoyment (*miqqa*), love as peaceful surrender (*istikana*), love as intimacy (*oulf*) and love as seduction (*foutoun*). There is of course love as intercourse (*nikah*) and love as eroticism and licentiousness (*ibahi*). There is a word too for the prestige that a man draws from loving, and being in the company of, women (*tashbeeb*). *Shawq* has been likened to the Greek 'eros', 'insofar as it was taken [by the mystic Muhyieddeen Ibn Arabi] as a fundamental driving force within human life, art, and thought'.

The word *jawa* refers to the alternating states of hope and despondency that a lover endures. Love that leaves us terrified and transfigured is *wahl*, while *sabwa* denotes nymph love and love for a younger person – it comes from the root words *sabi* for boy and *sabia* for girl. Some words have dual meanings, one of which works to reinforce the other: *jounoun* is both madness and love-as-madness – hence the famous Majnoun of Leila, also known as Qays. *Lathaa* is the way a flame audibly climbs up and consumes a dry piece of bark, but also means scorching love; *halaak* is extinction as well as fatal love.

In a surviving compendium of around 7,000 books from tenth-century Baghdad – called *Kitabu'l Fahrast*, compiled by Abu al-Faraj Ibn al-Nadeem, and providing a snapshot of medieval Arabo-Islamic literature – 'no less than a hundred (are about) love'.

I don't recall as a child ever hearing my mother or father, uncles or aunts, sisters or brothers, telling me 'I love you'; neither was I expected to say it. In the world in which I grew up, only lovers on TV or cinema screens said those words to each other. But I never felt the need for such direct assertion, because I never doubted that my family loved me. Love was conveyed to me in little gestures, subtle dispositions, and dozens of other words – *habibi* (my dear or my love), *omri* (my life), *rouhi* (my soul), *albee* (my heart).

When addressing her children, my mother would routinely add *ti'borni* ('may you bury me', as in 'may you outlive me')

Cover page of manuscript of Kitabu'l fahrast by ibn al-Nadeem.

to her utterance. Inevitably, this over-the-top expression drew ridicule from her grown-up children. To be fair, it was just a culturally convoluted way of saying 'may you live long', a habit of speech my mother had acquired from her rural upbringing and never abandoned even after moving to the city. But we, her children, urban to a fault, would not let nuance ruin an opportunity for a laugh.

Terms of endearment were always said in passing, sometimes with a little irony – 'Pass me the salt, *ya rouhi*' – but without the slightest drama and, unlike 'I love you', never calling attention to themselves or trying to be at the centre of the utterance. They emanated from naturally fierce loyalties and were hardly noticed except in reflective hindsight.

So much so, 'I love you' has come to acquire a particular connotation in my mind – smaller, a little hidden, and living alongside its bigger, sweeter and more comforting sense. Hearing those words brings up the possibility of their negation, of growing out of a world of all-encompassing love. It is as though a fish is being reassured that there is plenty of water in the ocean, not to worry, and so is needlessly reminded that there is indeed a world out there made of air, one in which it would suffocate.

This loss of innocence is not, of course, necessarily bad. That water, air and love are not omnipresent, not to be taken for granted, is knowledge we all need to acquire as part of growing up and growing strong. Nevertheless, I have inherited from my childhood this residual sense that hearing the direct reassurance of love in words, soothing as it is, is also a reminder of the possibility of its deficit, of a certain fragility inherent to the utterance. It is as if 'I love you' is always followed by a 'but' – small, silent, but no less real.

# An Honourable Woman

My mother was married off at fourteen or fifteen, against her wishes, to my 23-year-old father, whom she would first meet a few days before their betrothal. The union had been engineered by their mothers. This was the late 1940s, in the village of Sh'hoor, in rural south Lebanon, twenty kilometres to the east of the ancient Mediterranean city of Sour, better known as Tyre in English.

My mother had started to wear a headscarf a year earlier, following the custom of what was a deeply conservative society. When a girl crossed the threshold of puberty – real or perceived – suitors started roaming and parental paranoia kicked in, two problems thought to be easily solved with a head cover signalling chastity and, even better, a quickly arranged marriage.

My mother's family clan was the Sharafeddine: *sayyeds*, descendants of the Prophet, which imparted a certain status in the Islamic world. But for women of her generation, the title was also a burden, aptly reflected by the designation *sharifa*, which signifies both 'honourable woman' and 'descendant of the Prophet' – a double meaning also present in its male counterpart of *sayyid*. And, just in case anyone forgot, the first half of the family name, *sharaf* – honour – was there to remind them. The family, needless to say, was big on honour.

Add to this that both my mother and father came from the clerical class of Shia *ulama*. These were family clans of some distinction – such as al-Amine, Shamsuddine, Mroueh and Sharara as well as Sharafeddine and El-Zein – who regularly sent some of their sons to centres of religious learning in the seminary city of Najaf in Iraq, acquiring upon their return the title of sheikh or *aalim*, loosely translated as learned man or scholar. The *ulama*, plural of *aalim*, performed religious duties, led prayers, offered believers day-to-day advice and wrote books of exegesis or poetry in their spare time; some were appointed judges by religious authorities. All in all, they acted as community leaders.

But it was to Sierra Leone, not Najaf, that my mother's father, Sayyid Mohammad, had migrated to seek his fortune, leaving it to his eldest brother, Sayyid Abdel Hussein, to pursue a more illustrious career. They were half-brothers on their father's side, but Abdel Hussein's mother was a Sadr, a family clan considered to be Iraqi Shia nobility, which gave him unambiguously higher status within his own family. By the end of World War I, he had become a spiritual leader of Jabal Aamel, as south Lebanon was known in those times, one of only two Lebanese *mujtahids*, the highest and most prestigious rank an *aalim* can reach in the Shia world.

When my grandfather migrated to Africa, sometime in the 1930s, it fell to my grandmother, Zaynab, to raise a family of five – my mother, her two older sisters and her two younger brothers. One day Zaynab spilt a boiling pot in the kitchen, burning herself and her youngest badly. The village doctor prescribed the wrong treatment and her baby boy died in agony a few days later. So traumatised was my mother by the horrific event, she could still relate it to me, eighty years later, with an excruciating level of detail.

Sayyid Mohammad had been back for a few years when my mother turned fourteen. Before returning from Sierra

Leone, he had promised his daughter's hand to a Lebanese acquaintance of his there. My thirteen-year-old mother was excited by the idea, entertaining, no doubt, dreams of adventure and travel by ship to Africa.

Her father took her discreetly to a daguerreotype shop in Tyre and a photo of her without a veil was taken, to be sent to her suitor in Sierra Leone. Word quickly reached Sayyid Mohammad's powerful brother, who instructed that the photo be destroyed – 'The Sharafeddines do not send photos of their unveiled daughters across the seas,' he was reported to have said. As it happened, the photo survived through the goodwill of another uncle of hers, Sayyid Abdallah, who had been entrusted with disposing of the photo but instead hid it away. His daughter would give it back to my mother many years later, by which time she had become a young woman, living in Beirut, and had long stopped wearing a head cover.

But while the photo survived, the matchmaking had been nipped in the bud. My grandmother too was dead set against the plan and for good reason. Her hapless husband had done it before. Eight years earlier, as my mother's eldest sister, Jameeleh, turned thirteen, he had sent word from Sierra Leone that she needed to get on a ship and join him, because he had arranged her marriage to an excellent prospect, a wealthy Lebanese expatriate of good character and gracious looks.

What he hadn't told either his wife or his daughter was that the groom was an old man. True, he had a certain charm for a quinquagenarian, but he was short-sighted, a little hard of hearing, and by and large showed his age. My mother's sister, finding herself in unfamiliar land thousands of kilometres from home, had no choice but to go ahead with the ceremonial betrothal, but she refused to sleep with her husband. When the couple visited Lebanon a few years later and my grandmother finally discovered the truth, she was so horrified by what her husband had done that she insisted that her daughter be divorced there and then. Jameeleh would go on to marry someone else closer to her age who lived in the same town, rather than on another continent.

It was little wonder then that, when my grandfather made another attempt at matchmaking a few years later, his wife was not just skeptical but hostile. My grandmother must have felt the urge to act quickly since my mother, as everyone agreed, was a beautiful girl, several suitors were interested and there was no telling what her father might do.

My father was an ideal match – in his early twenties, from a 'good' family of *ulama*, just graduated from a teachers' college, and known to be independent and capable. It helped that he belonged to wealthy, land-owning family clans on both sides. His late maternal grandfather had been a feudal overlord who 'owned' six villages – including Sh'hoor itself, where the union was concocted.

There was only one problem: my mother did not want to get married. 'What do they want from me? Why can't they leave me alone?' she complained to her friends.

But her parents insisted and soon my mother was on her way with a stranger she'd only just met. She moved to my father's village and went on to give birth to seven children, losing her first-born to a fever when he was not a year old. My father's job, as a school inspector working for the Ministry of Education, required them to move around, living in different villages in south Lebanon over a few years. So it was that, in a few shell-shocking years, my mother went through uprooting, matrimony, child-bearing and infant death, away from her own family, all before reaching the age of seventeen.

A few years into their marriage, they finally settled in Beirut. They were following in the footsteps of many of their compatriots: in post-independence Lebanon migrating to the cities for a better life had become the norm. They rented an apartment in Haret Hreik, in the southern suburbs, where I was born eight years later. My father completed a law degree and became a senior civil servant in the Lebanese public administration.

Soon after arriving in Beirut, my mother took off the head cover – like many of her peers, she was joining the swelling ranks of the newly urbanised middle classes, cherishing the more relaxed and outward-looking mores of the city. The modern world, as it were, had finally caught up with my parents and their life course started to merge with the one I was born into. My three sisters, unlike my mother, never wore a headscarf, completed their schooling at private Catholic schools, and went on to acquire university degrees.

My mother, right, aged 40, with my father's cousin Naziha and my youngest brother Hekmat (circa 1974).

But there was no happy ending for my mother and father. They would develop a tired fondness for each other while bickering into old age. Neither did my mother forgive her parents for the arranged marriage, and even less so my father. She continued to speak about the trauma of her teenage uprooting well into her eighties and, judging by the telling, time was not much of a healer – not for her and not where it mattered.

# Ya Haraam

The Arabic word for respect, *ihtiraam* (with a long a), applies to both men and women. And yet it is subtly gendered in that it comes from the root *hrm* (pronounced *haram*, with a strong h and very short vowels), a word which, in its most generic sense, refers to all women within a men's circle of protection, be they sisters, mothers, nieces or wives. It has given us *hareem* for concubines (translated as the English *harem*), but also *haraam* (with one short and one long a) for taboo or what is beyond the pale, forbidden, in all spheres of life and not just gender relations.

Traditionally, one of the most egregious forms of disrespect one can extend to a man is to violate his *hrm* through verbal insult, intrusion into their private space or, worse still, illicit sexual relations with them. But *haram* is most commonly encountered in the expression *ya haraam* – 'what a pity' – which can sometimes take on a sardonic tone, becoming 'the poor bastard' or even 'yes, sure, that's so terrible, isn't it' (implying that it is not at all).

# Phantasms

In 1972, I was nine when my thirty-something uncle Ahmad, my father's half-brother on his mother's side and his only sibling, was stabbed to death in an altercation outside the Beirut school of which he was the owner and principal. My uncle's last words in the ambulance transporting him to the hospital were: 'If I die, my killer's name is Hussein Shabshoul.'

The murder may have been premeditated, as it transpired that the killer was in love with my uncle's fiancée, had resented their union and was known to have threatened to kill his rival.

Ahmad was a kind and gregarious man, by posthumous reputation but also in the patchy memories I have of him. He used to give me a quarter-lira coin every time he came to visit – enough to buy a soft drink or a chocolate bar – and sometimes took my three teenage sisters out to the cinema. He was younger than my father by close to a decade and seemed more extroverted, more at ease in the world, than his older brother.

My uncle's murder was the first death of a loved one I had experienced and the first direct encounter with violence that I can remember. Over the following few days – among commiserating visitors in our living room in Beirut and in nocturnal talks with my sisters at bedtime – I heard the story of my uncle's death retold several times over, like a drawn-out incantation, compulsively recited, as if it was the only form of catharsis that we had access to.

At the funeral and for a few days afterwards, the children and teenagers – siblings, and a dozen or so close and distant cousins – related the story with a kind of fascination that might have seemed obscene to an adult.

*The perpetrator climbed over the school fence and waited for my uncle under the stairs, dagger in hand. No, Shabshoul caught my uncle outside the school gate, silly boy, stabbed him once in the abdomen, six times in the heart – no, twice in the back. My uncle collapsed and fought back, blood spurted out of his gash like a fountain, streamed over his clothes, splattered his killer's face, pooled around his legs. A djinn came to my uncle in the ambulance and took him away – no, it was the archangel Gabriel, not the djinn, you stupid girl, and my uncle was seen smiling by the ambulance men. He is, right now, on his way to heaven. Police caught the perpetrator on the scene and handcuffed him, let him go, never caught him in the first place. The president told his ministers that the killer must be brought to justice. One of my uncle's cousins has charged his gun with six bullets and is out looking for Shabshoul and will soon …*

With barely a day or two gone, there was already, in the children's confused accounts of the murder and its aftermath, something both gritty and phantasmagorical about it.

My uncle's killer fled the scene and was never caught. A story was heard a few weeks later alleging that he was hiding in the nearby Shatila refugee camp. Another rumour, related to me decades later by my mother, had him escaping to the Baalbek-Hermel region – a part of Lebanon known for drug running, tribal rules of allegiance and score settling that harked back to pre-modern times, and where law enforcement was weak. The perpetrator, it was said, had been given refuge by Sabri Hamadeh, a powerful politician from that area, one of the key figures of Lebanese independence from France in 1943, and several times the parliamentary speaker. My uncle's family clan, so the rumour went in my mother's telling, supported Kamel al-Assad, another powerful politician. It was well known that al-Assad was an arch foe (and, curiously, brother-in-law) of Hamadeh: hence, according to the tale, the latter's action. This was a highly implausible story, even by the loose standards of familial rumour mills.

On the other hand, we did learn with more certainty, more than two decades after the murder, that the perpetrator had met a violent death during the 1975-1990 civil war. We had no other details about this. We all drew some satisfaction from this footnote to the tragedy, as if my uncle's plea for justice in the ambulance had been answered at last.

I once heard my eldest brother telling the story of my uncle's death to a few friends at his house – this was a few years ago, more than forty years after the event in question. He concluded by saying with a smile that my uncle's murderer had later died in 'mysterious circumstances', implying jokingly a mafia-like capacity for retributive violence, which our family – as law-abiding and peaceably middle-class as they came – did not remotely possess.

# The God Years

*What will happen to my uncle's soul? Will his murderer be punished and by whom?* My uncle's violent death inevitably raised questions in the children's minds, about justice and the afterlife, a combination that led straight to Allah, for He was the one being that most personified the two.

From when I was five or six, my father had coached me in prayer and Quran reading, and answered my questions about God. I was the fifth child of six in my family, and my father was well in his forties before I reached the age of ten. Talking about God was the easiest way in which we could have flowing, philosophical conversations.

I must have had many questions, but one I remember today was about the nature of God. How come He was so merciful on one page, and so threatening and, well, merciless, on another? Why did it matter to Him so much that we should believe in Him? The afterlife in the Quran was first and foremost a reckoning, a 'weighing of good and bad deeds', a final stage in one's existence in which justice was dispensed and could no longer be avoided. What made the prospect that God might not exist so terrifying – as much as, if not more than, the end of life upon death – was the implied absence of justice.

But the calculus of Judgement Day was still baffling to me: how many good deeds made up for a bad one, and how did God ultimately decide our fate and whether we ended up in heaven or hell or some purgatory in between? Would my uncle's killer be punished on this earth or in the afterlife, in the *dunia* or *aakhira*, or both?

Neither was the timeline clear. Was each person judged upon their death, shortly after they were led by the angels to meet their Creator? Or did they have to wait until Judgement Day, a collective reckoning at the End of Time, in which the entire universe came to a justiciable end? I preferred this last option, not least because of its epic scale and communal nature – it's better, after all, not to have to face such a reckoning alone. But if so, what happened to the dead while they waited for their penultimate day in court? And if not, what exactly *is* the point of Judgement Day?

My father pointed me, repeatedly, to the *makkya* chapters of the Quran – the shorter, more lyrically evocative ones, with their otherworldly, eschatological concerns. The *makkyas* coincided with the early phase of the Prophet's mission, when he was in Macca, persecuted, accused of being a possessed poet, and his monotheistic message rejected and ridiculed. This was well before his triumphant entry into the Madina that would herald the *madeeniyya* part of the scriptures, in which rules and laws, power and government, became prevailing and, by and large, duller themes.

By contrast, the *makkyas*, suffused with apocalyptic imagery about the end of the world, resonated with my budding existential angst. It was these verses that I heard most in calls to prayers and Quranic recitations on special occasions, from festive *eids* to solemn funerals:

My father, my younger brother Hekmat (front) and myself.

*When the Sun ceases to shine*
*When the stars fall down, and the mountains are blown away ...*
*When the seas are set alight and men's souls are reunited ...*
*When the records of men's deeds are laid open*
    *and the heaven stripped bare*
    *When Hell burns fiercely, and Paradise is brought near*
    *Then each soul shall know what it has done.*

There is a haunting quality to Quranic verses in Arabic that is achieved partly through reiteration. Adjectives and statements often occur in pairs, as in the excerpt above. 'The Compassionate, the Merciful', 'You alone we worship, and to You alone we pray for help', 'the Mighty One, the Wise One'.

One of the cornerstones of Quranic style is the special structure Arabic reserves for the dual form – a feature that has been lost from many languages, including modern Indo-European languages, but which has been preserved in Arabic. Nouns in Arabic are gendered and, in addition to singular and plural forms, there is a dual form for pairs.

The word for 'traveller(s)' is 'mussaafir', 'mussaafiraan' or 'mussaafiroon', depending on whether the subjects are one, two or more males, respectively. The conjugation changes yet again if the subject is female: 'mussaafira', 'mussaafirataan' or 'mussaafiraat'.

While the Quran is full of stories – either at the forefront of some *suraat* or buried in sermons, parables, lessons, harangues and rules – it has no overarching plot and the accepted organisation of its chapters, in roughly descending order of length, offers no narrative thread that might help the reader navigate it. This makes it into a difficult book to read from cover to cover.

That missing reading anchor I found instead, courtesy of my father, in the mostly *makkya* verses towards the end of the book. I kept returning to them – reading or listening to their *tajweed* recitation. They offered me lyrical tableaux of upheaval and natural wonder, conveyed through intensely musical forms and the mesmerising recurrence of *aan, oon* and *aat*.

*By the Dawn and the Ten Nights*
*By that which is dual, and that which is single*
*By the night when it comes!*

The *makkya* verses did not answer my questions about God and the world. But there was something ancient, otherworldly and yet reassuringly familiar about them. A window through which I could safely contemplate, and come to terms with, the world and its persistent mysteries. A kind of home within home – the innermost chamber of a spiral shell – made up of words and freewheeling thoughts and, always, the benevolence of my father's gaze.

# Homemaking

My father was dealt unusual cards as a child. Shortly after his birth, around 1925 or 1926, his father, Sheikh Ali, contracted tuberculosis while swimming in the Euphrates. He was about 25 years of age, living and studying in the city of Najaf in Iraq to become an *aalim* – hence the honorific attached to his name.

The disease was highly infectious, proximity to others became dangerous and, as a result, my grandfather could no longer have children, at least for a while. He would need treatment for the rest of his life, which made it impossible to continue his studies. He returned to his hometown, in south Lebanon, where he could better manage his ailment. He spent time at the hospice of Bhannes, in Mount Lebanon; his symptoms lessened, and he went on to have a reasonably normal and highly active life. He would become a literary critic, a dissenting historian of the nascent Lebanese nation and, like most learned men of his generation of south Lebanese intellectuals, would also dabble in poetry. He would live to the age of 84, by which time he had become practically blind.

Not long after contracting the disease, he divorced his wife, my grandmother Um Hassan, in order to spare her the miseries of his sickened lungs – at least, this was the reason according to one version of the story. My grandmother returned, with her child, to her father's house in the village of Sh'hoor. My grandfather never remarried, and my father was destined to become an only child.

Except that, a few years later, Um Hassan caused a scandal in the family when she announced that she was marrying again. Retying the knot was not the problem – young, divorcee women often remarried and were even socially pressured to do so. Rather, it was the identity of the groom, a stableman in her father's estate, that caused a stir. Part of the job of the stableman was to provide transport to women in the household, on horseback or mules, and many opportunities for private encounters would have presented themselves.

Marriage across such a class divide was almost unheard of and made people uncomfortable. But what made my grand-mother's move more remarkable, and far worse in the eyes of most people who knew her, was that her new husband was already married with children. The union was foolish, the bride's extended family believed, and a recipe for unhappiness. And, given the class chasm between bride and groom, it reflected badly on them as well.

Um Hassan's father had died shortly before her divorce and her mother, who herself came from wealth, appears to have approved of her daughter's unconventional move.

My grandmother gave birth to one child with her new husband, my uncle Ahmad, who would grow up with his half-brothers and sisters in Sh'hoor. My father, on the other hand, had to return to his father's house in the village of Jibsheet when he turned seven, following prevalent rules of custody. For the following few years, he lived in an extended family with his father and grandparents, as well as some of his uncles and aunts and their children. Unlike his cousins, he had no mother from whom he could seek protection, while his father, burdened with illness, had little time for him. His paternal grandmother, a loving woman, stepped into the role somewhat, but not quite enough to make up for his loss.

A few years later, having achieved high marks in his final year of primary school, he needed to move from Jibsheet to a bigger town to attend high school – in rural south Lebanon in the late 1930s, under the French mandate, the education system was still under-developed. He first moved to the nearby town of Nabatieh, where he lived for a little while in the household of an aunt; and, later, to the city of Saida, where he became a boarder and – he once told me, though not quite in those words – was bullied quite badly.

Class prejudice affected my father's relationship with his mother and his half-brother, Ahmad. While he loved them both, as a young man he became increasingly embarrassed by their social milieu and would only reluctantly visit them in their house in Sh'hoor. The contempt with which his extended family in Jibsheet held his mother and her new husband, whom they'd never met, carried over to him somewhat.

My father, in other words, had two childhood houses, thirty kilometres apart, that he could conceivably have called home, but both came with strings attached and neither qualified as such, not quite. Homemaking must have been a lifelong project for him, one that started very early in life, and which he must have undertaken with a degree of urgency.

At the age of 23, he asked his mother to help him find a bride, against the wishes of his father, who thought that he was too young for marriage. But by then he wasn't on good terms with his father anyway. When he finally tied the knot, that ultimate gambit of homemaking, he would walk away with the unhappy bride that was my mother, travelling from his mother's village to his father's. It was as if the child in him was still trying to bridge, two decades later, the chasm created by his parents' divorce.

As for his mother and half-brother, my father would continue to see them and love them until the end of their lives. My uncle would ultimately move to Beirut and my father, urged on by their mother, would help him in making the move and settling in the city. It was my father – by then a mid-ranking civil servant at the Ministry of Education, with oversight of private schools – who suggested to my uncle that he should purchase and run a school as a way of making a living, and helped him in closing the deal. This was the very same school where, a few years later, Ahmad would be murdered.

# Classe Sixième

October 1974. The big day has finally arrived. I am now in *classe sixième*, the first year of high school, at the Grand Lycée in Ashrafieh. No more school uniform, thank you very much, because we are grown up now, eleven years of age no less. A thrill in the air, a palpable sense of anticipation. Different playground too. Mingling with the giants, staying away from the bullies and looking down on the midgets across the fence. A little scary but mostly exciting. Bigger kiosk, with more choice of snacks. Textbooks ever more colourful, tackling human anatomy and modern history and the world economy and physics.

I sit in the first row, next to Mona, a sweet and slight girl, possibly the only kid in class who's timider than me, though my glasses are no doubt thicker. We hit it off instantly and sometimes I steal glances at her yellow shirt from out of the corner of my eyes.

Our year is going swimmingly well as we grow into our high-school selves and begin to prosper. Mona and I have become comfortable speaking with each other. But three months before the summer vacation, on 13 April 1975, war breaks out. Within a few weeks, Grand Lycée, though a five-minute drive from my house in West Beirut, becomes unreachable because it is located in Christian East Beirut, on the wrong side of the new Green Line dividing the city. The year 1975 turns out to be my last time there.

When, two years later, I see Mona walking into my class in Lycée Abdel Qader in West Beirut, I am quietly overjoyed. It turns out we are from the same side of the city, and I can certainly do with one less complication in my life, especially of the Romeo-and-Juliet kind. It doesn't take me long, however, to discover that we have both turned into self-conscious teenagers, an affliction that lasts a few years and kills any prospect of easy conversation between us.

# A New Kid on the Block

Our first English lesson lives up to expectations when the teacher – a native English speaker, though we have no clue where from – strides energetically into the classroom, writes her name on the blackboard in gigantic letters – M I S S   S P E A R – says it out loud once, and starts speaking in English straight away. It's all gibberish to us. We shake our mystified little heads and smile politely. Who will have the guts to break it to Meess Spé-Yaare that she has walked into the wrong class, not the more advanced one she is surely after? Not me, not Mona.

As it turns out, she hasn't, and it is not long before we let ourselves be drawn into this strange language, replete with bizarre turns of phrase – *The weather is nice, isn't it? How do you do? I beg your pardon* – which, when translated literally into Arabic or French, yields mostly laughter and not much by way of enlightenment. Besides, English pronunciation seems to bear no relation to its written form, as if a group of syllables have gone rogue, refusing to abide by the rules of language known to us. Either that or someone has accidentally run a batch of French words through an industrial meat mincer, then hastily put the maimed syllables back together.

All of which, after the initial shock of the first lesson, we begin to find delightfully exotic, and a welcome digression from French and Arabic. It isn't long before Miss Spear becomes one of our favourite teachers.

# Bullet, Paper, Rock

On 9 April 1973, an Israeli military unit sailed to Beirut and, using Zodiac speedboats, landed onshore at Ramlet'l Bayda – the White Sand beach – in the dead of night. Its members then killed three Palestine Liberation Organization (PLO) leaders in the residential neighbourhood of Verdun, where I once went to primary school. The events of that night became known in Lebanon as the Verdun Operation.

The raid was in revenge for the Munich attack that killed eight Israeli athletes in 1972. That attack had been staged by Black September, an organisation which the Israeli government alleged was run by the PLO leadership. A year earlier, the Palestinian novelist and member of the Popular Front for the Liberation of Palestine Ghassan Kanafani, and his seventeen-year-old niece Lamees Najim, were incinerated by a bomb planted by Mossad in the former's Austin 1100 in a suburb just outside Beirut.

To get from Ramlet'l Bayda to their targets – about a five-minute drive – the assassins used cars provided by embedded spies. In addition to the Palestinian leaders, they killed several victims unrelated to their primary targets, including an old Italian woman who, upon hearing the commotion, had come to check on her Palestinian neighbours. Ehud Barak, the future prime minister of Israel, led the attack. Decades later, by which time he had become an ex-prime minister, he related the operation cheerfully to a documentary maker, including how his team of assailants shot dead one of their targets, Youssef Al Najar, in his bedroom, along with his wife. The Israeli army called the operation Spring of Youth and its perpetrators were celebrated as heroes in Tel Aviv.

Six months later, at dawn on 6 October 1973, Egyptian commandos would cross the Suez Canal on Zodiac speedboats and launch a surprise attack on Israeli positions in the Sinai desert – occupied by the Israelis since 1967 – starting the October War.

But it wasn't until five years after the Verdun Operation that the PLO retaliated with a coastal landing of its own. On 11 March 1978, a group of *fedayeen* alighted on a beach near the kibbutz of Maagan Michael, north of Tel Aviv, using – irony no doubt intended – Zodiac speedboats. They hijacked a civilian bus on the coastal road and headed towards Tel Aviv. A gun battle with Israeli security forces ensued. Thirty-eight Israeli civilians, including thirteen children, were killed. The terrible toll would not diminish the glorification of the attackers as heroes among Arab supporters of the Palestinian cause. The PLO took responsibility for the attack and named it after one of its leaders killed in the Verdun Operation. A few days later, the Israeli army invaded south Lebanon.

I was ten at the time of the Verdun Operation, and I still remember the shock in the city the next day, with black-and-white photos splashed across newspaper front pages of bullet-ridden dead bodies in ordinary-looking rooms with frayed curtains and unmade beds. The government of the Sunni prime minister Saeb Salaam would resign, and the long-simmering tensions between the PLO and the Lebanese army would rise, because of the suspicion – not backed by evidence but not entirely unfounded – that the latter did not do enough to thwart the attack, and that the

Lebanese Second Bureau, the intelligence services close to the Maronite presidency, may have even colluded in the raid. (By the end of the decade, some Maronite politicians were openly collaborating with the Israeli state.)

Black September – the name of the organisation responsible for the 1972 Munich attack – was a reference to the bloody conflict, in 1970, that had pitted the PLO against King Hussein of the Hashemite Kingdom of Jordan, at the end of which the former was expelled from Amman. There was now a sense that the relationship between the Palestinians and their Lebanese hosts was deteriorating fast, just as it had in Jordan.

The premonition would soon be confirmed: in February 1975, a group of subsistence fishermen led by the charismatic left-wing Sunni leader Maarouf Saad marched through the streets of Saida. They were protesting the government's intention to grant monopoly fishing concessions to the firm Protéine, which was owned by Camille Chamoun, the right-wing Maronite politician, ally of the United States and former president.

It was hard enough, they argued, to make a living from the paltry catch they took from the sea using their primitive vessels and tattered fishing nets, without the government placing restrictions on their trade. The Lebanese army confronted the marchers; Saad was shot and later died from his wounds. The country was on tenterhooks and, five weeks after Saad's death, the Lebanese civil war broke out, on 13 April, pitting a coalition of PLO and pro-Palestinian left-wing progressives – mostly, though not exclusively, Muslim – against conservative Lebanese nationalists, Maronite Christian militias and sections of the Lebanese army.

Seven years later, the PLO leadership, including Yasser Arafat, would leave Lebanon, sailing across the Mediterranean to

Tunisia, expelled this time by the Israelis. The Lebanese civil war would run for fifteen years and go through several different phases, churning out new actors as others left the stage. It drew in foreign armies – Syrian, Israeli, Saudi, American, French, Italian – kept flaring up in new places around the small country and escalated along new fault lines.

But there was one abiding feature, almost always present in the background or at the forefront of events, and that was the Mediterranean. A stretch of a hundred or so kilometres of shoreline, in particular, had become the site of barely believable levels of violence over the last half a century. It started furthest south in Tyre, where a suicide bomber in 1982 brought down the building housing the Israeli occupation headquarters in the city, killing scores of Israeli soldiers and some of their Lebanese and Palestinian prisoners. It continued north towards Damour, a sleepy costal town, where in 1976 Palestinians and leftist fighters massacred a group of unarmed Christian civilians, while others fled north on hastily assembled boats. It reached Khaldeh, the point at which the coastal road turned west towards Beirut, where a fierce battle unfolded in 1982 between the PLO and the invading Israeli army, the latter helped by gunboats pounding the coastline. And only a few kilometres away, not long after, the Israeli army surrounded the Sabra and Shatila Palestinian camps, and invited their Christian militia allies to move into the camp – upon which they went on a killing spree, taking the lives of over a thousand unarmed civilians, including women and children.

It ran via the Ouzai slums, past the seaside airport, where the US army barracks were bombed, with 241 marines killed in 1983 – the mushroom cloud I saw from my south-facing French window was the first indication that this was no ordinary explosion. Past Ramlet'l Bayda, the not-so-leisurely beach where the French lost 58 soldiers on the same day and where, ten years earlier, the Israeli assassins had landed.

It rose up the Raouche cliffside road, with its once-fancy hotels and seedy bars, then snaked towards the Manara Corniche – so called on account of its lighthouse, bombed by the Israelis in 2006.

Halfway down the corniche one could find, until recently, a nondescript car park, where a building has now risen, and where the American Embassy once stood before it was brought down by a car bomb in 1979. And it was on the wide footpath of the corniche's famous promenade, lined with palm trees, that five years later solitary fishermen could be seen throwing their rods into the water while, on

Manara lighthouse in Beirut.

the far horizon where the sun would soon be dipping into the water, the *USS New Jersey* battleship shimmered as it launched one missile after another. It had been targeting a Druze militia in the Lebanese mountains, in a doomed effort by the Americans to prop up the regime of Ameen Gemayel, and the crumbling order that they and their Israeli allies had helped set up a year or so earlier.

The fishermen watched and fished, seemingly unperturbed, as if the war was a silly game that was no concern of theirs, trusting that American military technology was precise enough and that, since they were standing just outside the campus of the American University of Beirut, known as AUB, they must be safe because surely the Americans would not be so foolish as to bomb their own. As if a mere adjective was enough to confer the identity of one place, America, onto another, a stretch of land in West Beirut.

And it was on the corniche and close by, in and around the AUB campus where I was studying in the 1980s, that much of the saga of Western hostages would play out. I was on campus in 1984 when word spread that, an hour earlier, a man had walked into the office of the university president, Malcolm Kerr, in College Hall, and shot him point blank with a silencer-equipped gun. What I remember most was how otherwise ordinary that particular day was, how incongruous the murder was next to the uneventfulness of our lives on that week – assignments due, drinks to be had and movies to be seen. We gasped at the news, could barely believe it – it happened right next to us, and yet we hadn't seen or heard the shot and how could that be.

The coastal violence continued past Ain'l Mraisse and the beach resort of St George, to the site of the assassination of prime minister Rafic Hariri in 2005 by a massive bomb, first believed to be the work of Syrian intelligence but later blamed by an international tribunal on a Hezbollah operative. Into the red-light district of Zaytouneh – business not exactly booming ever since it became a no-man's-land at the start of the civil war and what's a brothel without men – right up to the doomed Beirut Port and the Dawra district to the north, neighbourhood of choice for successive waves of migrants, from Armenia to Sri Lanka and the Philippines, and site of petrochemical storage that more than once burst into flames, because of air bombing or poor maintenance, blanketing the city with black smoke. And not far from here was the old Quarantine district and the Tal al-Zaatar Palestinian refugee camp where, early in the war and on more than one occasion, Christian militiamen went on murderous rampages. Further north is Zouk Mikael, the small town where a bomb planted at a church in 1990 killed eleven and injured more than fifty, a crime for which a Christian warlord spent several years in jail, although his supporters believed he was framed.

Some of the most memorable spectacles of violence played out on this coastal stretch, stacking up at uncanny speed, overwhelming our collective ability to make sense of events and challenging our capacity to remember and, even more gravely, our need to forget. It imparted to us a kind of a stoicism, a weary form of maturity, regardless of how young or old we were.

What I, and many of my fellow Lebanese, witnessed over the years refused to fit into the mental construct offered by those who had taken the time to reflect on violence, be it Frantz Fanon upholding its virtues or Hannah Arendt condemning its perniciousness. Violence on our shores seemed neither to 'detoxify' the poison of colonial subjugation, as Fanon argued – it might have in the mind of its perpetrators, but if so, it also created new contamination – nor to overwhelm the ends to which it had been deployed, as Arendt believed: it was often remarkably successful at achieving its ends and converting itself into lasting power.

Beneath the seemingly chaotic mess of bloodshed, there was method to the madness. Early on in the war, two dynamics emerged. The first was typical of civil warfare between factions more or less equal in power, battling it out across difficult-to-change front lines, with mostly light and medium-range weaponry – automatic guns, rocket-propelled grenades and mortar shelling. But from 1976, when the Syrian state first intervened in the war, followed two years later by the Israeli army, a new dynamic emerged. Invaders with access to more advanced technologies and regular fighting forces came by land and sea, and some locals fought them onshore while others welcomed them, though never for long. Israelis, Syrians, Saudis, Americans, French, Italians. The battleship against the car bomb. Guerrillas taking on tanks. Marines facing suicide bombers. Abuses rife on all sides.

What this motley of warring actors shared, for all their heterogeneity, was what Walter Benjamin called 'a doubleness in the function of [military] violence': namely, violence as both law-breaking, aiming to overcome a legal order erected by one's enemies, and law-preserving, defending one's own legal order. The shifting ground of the fightings in Lebanon was such that it was never entirely clear, at any point in time, who was pursuing which of these two motivations.

It was as if an asymmetry of power between East and West, North and South, had crystallised along a liminal strip of the Beirut shoreline where I happened to be growing up, by a peculiar accident of history and geography. Only later, well after war shoved me from childhood into teenage life, would I come to understand that perhaps this formative experience was less accidental, more probable, than I had first thought – even a little preordained. That the Mediterranean was as much a site of conflict and a source of fear as a space of leisure, trade and exchange. That the seeming peacefulness of its shimmering waters, at dawn and dusk and in between, made its menace all the greater. Perhaps that day in Saida when, still a child, I almost drowned in it was not so much a story of hero-rescues-boy as an early warning of things to come.

# TWO: YOUTH

# The Karate Years

I once developed a keen, if short-lived, interest in karate. I was fourteen and had been a fan of Bruce Lee for some time. I had watched all his movies, several times over, at least the ones that had made it to the Carmen or the Salwa, two downmarket cinemas in the working-class neighbourhood of Mazraa in Beirut, a ten-minute walk from where I lived. *Enter the Dragon, Way of the Dragon* and *Fist of Fury* are the ones I still remember but there must have been others.

My interest in martial arts was not sophisticated – I never gained more than the vaguest understanding of the differences between karate, kung fu and taekwondo. And yet I could mimic, with impressive accuracy, some of the moves and kicks of Bruce Lee, including the machine-like, torsional movement of one of his arms, thrusting forward, fist closed, while the other arm cranked back synchronously, his eyes looking sideways, in a half-mad, half-shrewd kind of way, keeping everyone on edge, opponents and viewers alike. But my best work, by far, was in replicating the strangely modulated sounds that came out of his mouth and which, sometimes, as they rose towards the highest soprano, seemed to be having a more effective psychological impact on his foes than his flying acrobatics.

When a karate academy handed out leaflets outside our school in the Mar Elias neighbourhood, two of my classmates enrolled. One day, at recess, they took out the crisply ironed uniforms from their backpacks, and unfolded them for our benefit, including the white, yellow and orange belts, all of which had been handed out to them upon registration. They showed off their skills and spoke about martial arts with the inviolate authority imparted by the one and a half lessons they had completed so far – apparently, the teacher was sick halfway through the second lesson and had to go home. We examined the thick fabrics, fascinated and envious, feeling with our fingers, sniffing the starch, admiring the colour rainbow, and wistfully visualising ourselves as karate champions.

BRUCE LEE

FURY OF THE DRAGON

Starring BRUCE LEE - VAN WILLIAMS · Produced By L.L. & J.M.J. ENTERPRISES
Executive Producer LAURENCE JOACHIM · Directed By WILLIAM BEAUDINE · Music By AL HIRT

I resolved, there and then, to enrol too. The problem was that not only was there a cost involved, but a substantial down-payment too, and my father was the only source of income I had access to. Now, my father's track record in supporting expensive extracurricular activities for his six children was nonexistent. This was perfectly understandable in retrospect, given our rather large family but, as a teenager, I saw it as bitterly unjust. So I did my homework before approaching him, developing what I thought was a convincing argument and a strong negotiating position.

As a child, I had watched my father do some haggling in the souks of Damascus and was always impressed, if a little embarrassed, by his wild gambits. To the two hundred Syrian lira demanded by the seller for a precious piece of fabric or a tea service, he would not hesitate in offering twenty and I, listening, would feel my cheeks go red and wish the ground would swallow me.

It didn't help that my father had a knack for mimicking the Syrian accent when in Syria – and no doubt the Egyptian one in Cairo and the Palestinian in Ramallah. It wasn't deliberate, I think, and came naturally to him. But as I listened to him speaking to Syrians in Syria, I feared that his interlocutors might construe it as mockery, take offence and say something mortifying in return, because the Lebanese sometimes mimicked Syrian accents in jest among themselves.

On the contrary, more often than not, my father would leave on excellent terms with the shopkeeper, after completing the transaction at a price not far above his own initial offer. This may or may not have involved, halfway through the protracted negotiation, my father staging a walk-away, which would trigger a mini-chase by the vendor or his fetch boy and a significant shift in my father's favour. Occasionally, of course, the vendor would remain unmoved,

I suspect pleased to see the back of us, and we would just keep walking. When this happened, my father, to his credit, never returned, even when he was keen on the item in question.

It was a different story in the more upmarket shops of Beirut where my father sometimes took us to buy shoes, clothes or books, in the Hamra or Ashrafieh districts. There, haggling was frowned upon, and my father was more restrained, although he couldn't resist it sometimes, casually throwing 'I'll pay you half of that' or 'is this your final price?', usually to the visible annoyance of curt saleswomen. My embarrassment, in such instances, though still a case of teenage prudishness, was more well-founded.

With hindsight, I came to admire my father's haggling skills and insistence on doing things his own, old-fashioned way, unfazed by the modern norms of his city. There was a lesson here for me, one that I came to understand only later in life, about the inherent malleability of the world, its negotiability, about the way we approach boundaries and lines in the sand and how we judge them. It was a dangerous lesson in some ways – some boundaries may not be as malleable as they appeared or, even more dangerously, should not be as malleable as they were – but a useful one, nonetheless, that I carried with me.

In order to pursue my novel martial-arts ambition, and before talking to my father about it, I calculated the full expense for a year – down payment plus monthly fee – and came up with a cost-sharing scheme, drawing on the full might of my weekly allowance. True, my contribution was paltry, even after exhausting my pocket money for a year, but I was willing to dip into my income from the following year, going into debt as it were, and that was a hell of a trump card, I thought, to play at the right moment in the negotiation, and only if required – the equivalent of the paradigm-shifting walk-away gesture in the souks of Damascus.

Given the age difference between me and my father, as well as the disparity in purchasing power, my contribution, while the smaller of the pair by far, was still quite respectable, I believed. The mere suggestion of it, I had hoped, might shame my father into acquiescence. He was, after all, a man with a taste for negotiation, I reminded myself for encouragement: not only might he ultimately agree to my generous offer but, who knows, in a moment of fortitude I knew he was capable of, he might volunteer to cover the full cost and spare me the indignity of going without pocket money for quite some time.

What I got instead, after two weeks of toing and froing, was the paradigm-shifting *inshallah*. I first approached my father about the matter one night, at a carefully chosen time, half an hour before the evening TV news, which I knew would monopolise his attention for most of the evening. He heard me out and asked me a few questions – how many times a week were lessons and where was the academy located, how would I get there and how much it all cost – and then said that he would think about it. I left it a few days and asked him again. He said it was expensive and the logistics were inconvenient. I told him I was prepared to contribute from my pocket money, and that I would get myself there and back under my own steam and he need not worry about this. He said he still wanted to think about it.

When I broached the subject two days later – Are you going to let me do those karate lessons, Dad? – he looked at me in silence for a moment and said *inshallah*. A week later, same answer, by which time, as my father knew, it was getting late for enrolment, and I had already missed several lessons. *Inshallah* was my dad's way of saying no. I walked away and never raised the matter with him again.

No word irritated me more than *inshallah* in those days. It was a contraction of a three-word expression, *in shaa'a llah*, 'if God wills (it)', and its abbreviated form, if anything, made it far too easy to throw around in everyday language. *Inshallah*, as far as I was concerned, was the height of hypocrisy: men using the pretext of God's will to further their own or, worse, hiding behind God to avoid justifying their actions. Far from being a sign of fatalism among Arabs and Muslims, as it was sometimes construed by outsiders, it was the expression of human will at its canniest and, from my point of view, most exasperating. My resentment at being denied became focussed on this one word, as though it were a talisman – if, somehow, I could banish it from the Arabic dictionary, then everything in the world would fall into place.

I never took karate lessons and my martial-arts phase, including the movies of Bruce Lee, faded shortly after. But *inshallah* grew on me over the years. Perhaps I was bound to become more amenable to it as I acquired more independence, left behind my powerlessly desiring teenage self, and the expression no longer had the same effect on me. Whatever the case may be, I came to see a more philosophically appealing side to it.

*Inshallah*, I now understood, could teach me something about desire, at the precise moment of its denial, one which the word itself has been entrusted to convey. By bringing God into a transaction in which He seemingly had no business, it reminded me that there was another world beyond my own, in which my desire, and the pain that comes with it, fades into insignificance. It told me tacitly that the renunciation the world was demanding of me may not be such a bad thing after all. And while I might resist this avenue of thinking for a while, it was there for me to seize upon when I was ready for it.

Besides, not only was *inshallah* a gentler, more playful way of saying no, it conveyed a different kind of no altogether. It was a form of negation that tacitly argued against its own finality, allowing for a window of hope, softening the disappointment and reminding the boy at the receiving end that nothing was immutable about the world except God and that God wrought miracles after all.

# Tell Tales

Haani falls in the playground and bangs his head on the pavement. He's conscious and strangely silent. A teacher squats on the ground next to him, places the injured head in his lap, and presses against the cut with the palm of his hand to stem the bleeding. An ambulance comes blaring through the metal gate, medics load him onto a stretcher and take him away. The ambulance has barely disappeared when rumours start rushing in, like blood towards the locus of trauma.

X-ray taken. Concussion diagnosed. In a critical state. Home this afternoon. Taken to AUH Hospital. Gash sewn shut. Forty-four stitches like the centipede. X-ray negative. No concussion. In intensive care at Maqassed Hospital, just for observation until tomorrow. In a stable condition. Haani, stable? Is that even possible? And yes, seven stitches, that's all. Not ten, not twenty and certainly not forty-four. Seven, like the seven wonders of the world.

The principal gathers those of us who claim to have seen what happened, in the shade of the oak tree, behind the snack kiosk, fourteen- and fifteen-year-old boys and girls from *quatrième* and *troisième* classes. A ten-year-old kid thinks he can join us, but we quickly disabuse him of such a notion.

There is hierarchy in the telling and the listening. Subtle and not so subtle. We scan the principal's face and closely follow her gestures, desperate for attention – a nod here, a slight turn of the head there, the hint of a smile or a raised eyebrow and, most of all, her forefinger pointing this way and that.

I know everything with certainty. That Haani had been running towards the water fountain when he tripped on the almost-invisible, criminally unnecessary step and fell. That he hadn't been pushed by anyone. I would offer his propensity to overload his school bag and the unsteadiness of his gait as contributing factors. I would mention his parents' divorce, last year, by way of background.

I have an idea or two about how to prevent such misfortunes in the future – the fall, not the divorce. The stupid step to start with and, while we're on this, why not fix the broken window with the jagged edge in *classe troisième*, which surely is an accident waiting to happen. And then there is the seemingly unrelated, but arguably important, matter of ...

Not ideal that I have to tender my account in French to our French principal. I would have preferred Arabic, but never mind, French will do and I am sure I can pull it off. First, though, I have to jostle through the verbal crowd and make myself heard over other boys, bullies and busybodies. I am competing against other stories and Mme Vieillard, sadly, has only two ears, if that, and little time to spare.

Before I know it, before I can get so much as a sigh in, let alone a word, the principal is on her way back to her office – grey hair pulled back in a bun, dark-blue dress flapping at her calves, shoes click-clacking away – satisfied with the accounts of one or two loudmouths.

Speaking truth to power, someone said, huh? Well, good luck getting a hearing.

# Tiptoeing around Desire

If *inshallah* tormented me in an underhanded way, *saree'l atab* made no bones about its hostile intentions. This formal Arabic expression gave me some grief in my teenage years in the mid-1970s. It can be translated, loosely, as 'quick to succumb (to sexual desire)'. I had come across it on TV and in newspapers, courtesy of commentators criticising the proliferation of semi-pornographic ads in Beirut, on billboards and in the windows of movie theatres. The experts – conservative pundits, and Christian and Muslim clerics alike – were calling for the ads to be taken down, professing to be concerned about their effects on *saree'l aatab* young men.

I would have been about thirteen and, unbeknown to me, my hormones must have been in hyperdrive. Unbeknown because, apart from a one-off conversation with a cousin of mine in which he told me how babies were made, about the only sex education I had received at that time were the obscenities I had heard in the school playground and during the street fights I had witnessed. *Ayree bi immak,*– 'my dick in your mother' (why anyone would want to do that was beyond me), or the more factual *kiss ikhtak akhou sharmouta,* 'your sister's cunt (is the) brother of a whore' (a baffling kinship, and why would the female sexual organ be masculine, and how can they tell anyway).

Needless to say, the passing exclamations did not much enlighten me on matters of sex. Connoisseurs of Arabic swearing might point out that a more accurate translation of the last insult is 'your sister's cunt, (you) brother of a whore' but try telling a literal-minded teenager desperately trying, and mostly failing, to decipher the many mysteries of his own little cosmos.

Given the socially conservative world in which I was growing up, those much-maligned ads were about the only sexual outlets available to me. And I would have been happy to indulge in the secret voyeurism that the larger-than-life posters afforded me – a skimpy dress here or the hint of a breast there. I would have continued to go with friends to the cinema and watch titillating movies, some of which, though considered beyond the pale back then, might pass muster as family entertainment today.

I would have kept wishing for that Beiruti teenage urban myth, *aatshe abu khalil*, to be true: the promise that Abu Khalil – the generic name of all sleazy movie-projection men – might insert a hardcore sex act in the middle of a totally unrelated movie. The Abu Khalils of the world were said to possess a dozen gems of short-reel pornographic strips, cut off longer movies and hidden from the censor, which they would occasionally splice into another full-length movie, to the delight of their audience of mostly pimpled teenagers and a few older men.

Sadly, I only experienced the salacious intercession once, in a dodgy backstreet cinema while watching a World War II drama. I say sadly because I was enjoying the movie, the interposed extract was more tasteless than arousing and I was annoyed by the crude directorial licence of my Abu Khalil of the day. The aesthetic case against porn, I decided, responding to the pundits babbling in my head, was perhaps even stronger than the moral one.

In any case, I would have ignored the preaching experts altogether, as well as my own confusion, and would have kept consuming whatever the city offered me by way of sexual excitement, scant as it was. I would have carried on glancing at the ads when I could and watching the occasional sleazy Italian movie, with titles such as *The Nurse* and *Private Lessons*, never mind the insufferable plots and dreadful acting. I would have continued to catch those episodes of *I Dream of Jeannie* that featured regularly on our TV and which I now saw in a different light, especially those in which the ever-flirtatious Barbara Eden wore titillating outfits – from her trademark midriff-baring gilet to the skimpy tennis dress reaching to only just below the groin.

But *saree'l aatab* preyed on my mind. Though uttered in an ostensibly sympathetic tone – those poor *saree'l aatab* young men need our protection – it was condescending, accusatory and guilt-inducing. It evoked other words such as feeble, spineless, sex-crazed, silly and obsessed. After all, the root word *atab*, meaning breakdown, malfunction or flaw, has also given us *maatoub*, as in mindless, idiotic, inane. Add to it the terrifying urban myths, endemic to Beirut's youth, about *al'aada'sirrya*, the secret habit – how onanism will make you blind, deaf and mentally deranged, not to mention the myriad forms of torture it will earn you in the afterlife.

Am I *saree'l ataab*? The question worried me for a few months. Was I alone in reacting to those images the way I did? In my less cheerful moments, I imagined my 'normal' peers effortlessly, heroically brushing aside the images. Now, asking my peers was out of the question, of course. But on the positive side, some of those peers were not very good at hiding their reactions – a comment here, a passing remark there, a keenness to watch some of those same movies. The world's thick veil of mystery, I realised, was not entirely opaque. And so I reached a temporary compromise with myself: I didn't know whether I was *saree'l aatab* or not, whether I was so deficient there was a word in the language to describe my flaw, but even if it turned out that all this was true, I knew that I was not alone in suffering from the condition, and in this I found a most comforting consolation.

# Conditional Fluency

My French is fluent except when I am speaking to our French school principal, Madame Vieillard, or the equally French vice-principal, Monsieur De Bon. I am puzzled by this. True, Mme Vieillard is an intimidating woman and the decline in my fluency may be nothing more than a dip in my self-confidence. But what about Monsieur De Bon, our vice-principal, a man as gentle as they come?

I know the words, but they seem to fail me in the moment when I need them most. I feel beset by *l'esprit de l'escalier* – literally, 'the spirit of the stairs' – that delightful French metaphor referring to a dinner-party guest, in the stairwell about to leave her host's house, when the witty retort to something that was said to her a few minutes earlier finally, mortifyingly, occurs to her.

In time, I would come to understand the source of my oral difficulty by reading Pierre Bourdieu's *Qu'est ce que parler veut dire* (Language and Symbolic Power), with its trenchant analysis of the modes and subtleties of linguistic domination. Bourdieu's earliest sociological research was conducted among the Kabyles of French Algeria and his own working-class roots no doubt made him more sensible to the verbal intricacies of power dynamics. In the Pyrénées Aquitaine, where he grew up, the Béarnese dialect was widely spoken before it was displaced by the official French language in the nineteenth century, and this also informed his analyses, including ways in which resistance to dominant languages emerges.

But all these insights would come far too late for me: *Qu'est ce que parler veut dire* would only be published in 1982, two years after I left school, and I would only find out about it from an anthropologist friend of mine another forty years down the track.

*Le temps d'apprendre à vivre, il est déjà trop tard* – 'By the time one learns how to live, it is already too late' – said a song I often listened to in my teenage years, courtesy of yet another two Frenchmen, Georges Brassens and Louis Aragon. Decidedly, Francophonie is a comprehensive package of enlightened disempowerment.

# My Little rrr Problem

I have to make an oral presentation in *classe biologie*: I must stand in front of the class, next to my teacher, and read the few hundred words I have written about dissection and anatomy.

The problem in a nutshell: the 'proper' way of saying 'r' in French is 'gh', but most Lebanese tend to pronounce it as 'rrr'. *Ils roulent leur r*, it is said – They roll their r. 'Gh' is soft but guttural, produced by keeping one's tongue flat while sucking in air, as if one is about to do some gargling. 'Rrr', on the other hand, is made by expelling air with the tongue bent sharply upwards, touching the palate and causing vibration around the lower lip. The verdict in the playground is unambiguous: 'gh' is effete, 'rrr' is manly. It goes without saying.

One has to choose, and there are costs and benefits either way. I like to think of myself as scientific and wish to speak French with precision, as the French do. Which leaves me lying on a rock, staring at a hard place: say 'gh' and earn an aura of Gallic sophistication, and a pat on your shoulder from your teachers, but be prepared to live with the mockery of your peers, who see only affectation, not linguistic skill.

I fall on the time-honoured solution developed by that most curious of species of lizards, the *chamaeleonidae*:

I adjust according to my audience at any particular moment, achieving a satisfying level of authenticity in the process.

There remains the not inconsiderable problem of mixed audiences – in class, when one is called on to speak in the presence of both teachers and classmates. For my afore-mentioned biology presentation I consider mixing my rs, using 'gh' in one sentence and rolling them with abandon in the next, catering to conflicting demands. But in doing so I may end up pleasing no one. There is no getting around it: I must go one way or another. I opt for 'gh': of the two authorities bearing down on me, the teacher's is surely more consequential.

When my name is called, I get up, piece of paper in hand, walk to the front of the room, stand facing the class next to the teacher and, with some trepidation and much resolve, deliver in the way I have set out to. I am a little too self-conscious about my pronunciation, but my rs are so admirably French, part of me is already clapping. So much so, I am mostly oblivious to the content of what I am reciting. When I complete my speech, the teacher tells me that the research is good but my delivery is too mechanical.

On the positive side, I experience no repercussions for my linguistic sell-out. In fact, I discover over the next few days that my peers and I are rather tolerant of one another's quirks in class, provided that, in each other's company, we double down on rolling our rs, performing our Lebaneseness with gusto.

# Tribes in Trouble

One day in 1979, a burly geography teacher at my high school – one of three Mission laïque française schools in Beirut – slapped a student in my year, in reaction to some impertinence on the student's part. I was in *classe seconde* (year 10), and the city had recently emerged from civil war into a state of quasi-normality; but the rule of law had not been entirely re-established, political violence was creeping up again and, though we didn't know it, war hadn't really ended, and many cycles of violence were still to come.

Naturally, our solidarity went to our peer, against this crude exercise of authority. The teacher in question was Monsieur Bogart, a balding, slightly overweight Frenchman, who seemed always to wear the same faded beige corduroy suit, did not connect well with his students and, as far as we were concerned, lived at the opposite pole on the charisma scale as his Hollywood namesake.

We were further outraged when the redoubtable Madame Vieillard (Ms Oldy) and Monsieur De Bon (Mr The Good) refused to treat the matter with the gravity it deserved. Inevitably, the incident acquired a bitter colonial flavour, and hence stirred even stronger emotions than it might have done otherwise. With a different state of mind, and some distance from the events, we might have reacted differently.

We could have seen, for example, the satiric potential of the protagonists' names.

Corporal punishment was not unheard of, but it was rare and certainly did not occur in the school's senior classes. The only other memory I now have of physical violence exercised by teachers was from seven years earlier, back in primary school, where a certain Monsieur Berbéri seemed to enjoy picking on a rather placid kid, always the same one for some reason, handing down painful floggings to the hands with a ruler, in view of all the other students in the classroom, while tears streamed down the poor boy's face. We would watch in terror, our little minds desperate to make sense of the sadism of the man in whose care we had been placed, trying to find some reassuring justification in the boy's own behaviour; and yet, with all the psychological self-deception in the world, could never find it in ourselves to fault the victim.

My end-of-year class picture in classe huitième (year 5, primary school) with our teacher Monsieur Berbéri; I am in the back row, 3rd from the left.

On the day following the slapping incident, we decided to go on strike. We walked out of our classrooms in a co-ordinated action and assembled in the school playground. I was head of the student association and, together with my fellow association members, we put our demands to Madame Vieillard, not without trepidation: Monsieur Bogart must be disciplined and he must apologise to the student he assaulted.

I don't remember at what point we returned to our classes – we were probably on strike for no more than two or three days. We did not manage to extract any concession from the school, as far as I recall, which was not suprising given Madame Vieillard's contempt for the student body. In any case, the more interesting follow-up events occurred outside the school, not in the principal's office.

When our French literature teacher, Monsieur Soulier (Mr Shoe), a man we loved and admired, walked into the school on the first morning of the strike and queried us about the reason for our assembly, we expected him to be sympathetic. We had received quiet support from some of our Lebanese teachers at the school, and did not doubt that someone with Monsieur Soulier's intelligence and sensibility would extend his.

Monsieur Soulier wasn't just another teacher. For one, his lectures brought to life the poetry of Baudelaire and Rimbaud, and the prose of Flaubert, Proust and Huysmans. He had little time for boring curricula, and you never knew what he might talk about when he walked into the classroom on Monday morning, occasionally a little inebriated. One time he raged about a big-screen adaptation of *Madame Bovary* he'd seen the day before and which, deceived by advertising, had expected to be an arthouse movie but turned out to be soft porn, and how it ruined his evening, and why it's important to draw the line between eroticism, sensuality and pornography, and how best to tell the difference.

Another time he waxed philosophical about a female guest of his house who sat on a chair that was a work of art, not really a chair; one was supposed to admire it, not sit on it, though, at the same time, it *was* a chair, so he couldn't quite fault his guest; and what is art and what is not art, and does art serve a purpose or must it be useless by definition; and how can one tell the difference between the prose of Proust and that of an advertising pamphlet, and so on and so forth.

Monsieur Soulier was also the man who once, at a public lecture by a visiting French psychoanalyst in the Salle Montaigne of the French Cultural Centre on Damascus Road, reacted to a long-winded question by a young woman in the audience by yelling at the top of his voice, from his seat towards the back of the lecture theatre: '*Donnez-lui un divan.*' (Give her a [shrink's] couch.)

Though we felt sorry for Monsieur Soulier's target, we were awed by his audacity.

And, as if his sparkling intellect and natural charisma weren't enough, Monsieur Soulier drove a flash old sports car – a red convertible two-seater – and was regularly seen with one or two ravishing women. It was a case of cool dude meets Renaissance man – a larger-than-life character who had it all, as far as French-educated teenagers with intellectual aspirations were concerned. Male teenagers, at least: I don't remember what the girls in our classroom made of him.

But Monsieur Soulier, to our surprise, was unimpressed by our strike. He admonished us, insisting that we were being silly and irresponsible, that Monsieur Bogart was a troubled man, that our actions would lead to the slapping incident being written in his employment record, which would practically kill off his career, and that such an outcome would be far out of proportion with the offence. Come to think of it, Monsieur Bogart did cut a rather sad figure, but it was immaterial, as far as we were concerned, and nothing could justify his action.

Turning to the assaulted student himself, Monsieur Soulier suggested, his mischievous, tooth-gapped smile suddenly lighting up his face, that he should instead get even by scratching the bonnet of Monsieur Bogart's car, or puncturing its tyres, or whatever, and then forget the whole matter because, frankly, we've been blowing it out of all proportion.

Which is exactly what the student did, though going a little further: the thug hired to do the deed, a couple of weeks later, chased Monsieur Bogart down the street for about a hundred metres, as he ran at full speed towards the safety of the school premises.

The newly acquired athleticism of our geography teacher would become the merry talk of the school playground for a few days. That the student in question hailed from a part of Lebanon where people were known for not forgetting slights, and taking justice into their own hands, brought to the story a delicious local element.

As for Monsieur Soulier, we knew that he was anti-clerical, certainly not a turn-the-other-cheek kind of guy, but to hand out tooth-for-a-tooth practical advice to a bunch of boys in civil-war Beirut was an unbelievably delightful way of turning native. At the same time, his solidarity with his fellow Frenchman we found unabashedly tribal – further evidence that beneath the self-declared civilisational veneer of France lies something far cruder.

Our much-loved French literature teacher Monsieur Soulier.

Still, Monsieur Soulier's tolerance of some violence against his fellow Frenchman complicated the picture for our feverishly analytical minds. He had trained us in extracting counterintuitive meanings from subversive, proto-modernist texts: one student suggested that perhaps, in handing out his advice, Monsieur Soulier was just showing us how you can abide by a moral code and subvert it at the same time. Or perhaps, someone else offered, he was revealing the barbarism in every man and woman, not just the French. A most charitable interpretation, in retrospect.

Thinking today about the incident, I see two sides to it. The school was a relatively healthy space in which we were being initiated into power relationships, allowed to understand how we might survive them, prosper through them, perhaps even – with single-mindedness and a little help from history – transform them.

But it was also a world running in tension, one where it didn't take much for the powerful to resort to violence. Monsieur Soulier's solidarity with Monsieur Bogart may have been motivated by something as simple as friendship or sympathy for a troubled colleague. But it is hard not to suspect that what lay behind it, as well, was that most insidious of tribal solidarities, the one that united men in shared power, by virtue of class, race, gender or age. Or, in this case, possibly all of the above.

# Missed Appointment

It is the summer of 1980, my final year at school. War resumed a few months ago – this time between the Syrian army and the Christian militias of East Beirut – and it is uncertain whether or not the national baccalaureate exams will take place. Our house is too close to the Green Line, no longer safe, and we moved, two months ago, to my eldest brother's apartment, well inside West Beirut. There are too many of us for the two-bedroom flat, nine in total, and we have to sleep on mattresses.

I have to make do with a makeshift study desk on the balcony, the only space quiet enough for me to prepare for my exams, war or no war. I have to live with street noise but it's still better than the unending commotion inside the apartment. Besides, I have set up the desk against the wall, with my back always to the street to avoid visual distraction.

The last three weeks have been quiet, including at the front line, courtesy of a ceasefire and ongoing negotiations between warring parties to try to reduce tensions.

It's three o'clock in the afternoon. I have turned myself into a problem-solving automaton, tackling one maths exercise after another, from trigonometry and calculus to algebra and space geometry.

I get up to go the bathroom, fifteen seconds away. I have only just pulled up the toilet seat when an explosion shakes the building. I flinch and freeze, then, after a few moments, walk out of the bathroom. Everyone is shaken but safe. No one knows what it was. We all gather in the corner of the flat that is least exposed to windows and wait a little in case there is more to come. There isn't.

We walk out onto the balcony to find out what happened. The apartment is on the first floor, barely three metres above ground, and we see a small crater in the middle of the street. A lone shell has exploded right in front of the building, all the more eerie since there has been no fighting whatsoever.

As I turn around to walk back inside, I notice something near my desk: the part of the wall level with, and roughly half a metre above, my desk, is strewn with pockmarks from flying shrapnel. I don't need to be a ballistics expert to work out that, had the shell landed one minute earlier, or later, shards of hot iron would have cut through the base of my neck into the back of my skull.

# On Time

The driver of the shared car finally drops me at the school gate of Lycée Abdel Qader. We have been stuck in traffic and I am fifteen minutes late for class. Walking fast across the courtyard and into the building, I rehearse in my mind the excuse I am going to give Mr Raad, my Arabic literature teacher. I will say in my own defence that I have already finished the assignment we are discussing in class today. As I skip stairs towards the second floor, it hits me that there is no word for 'already' in Arabic. I could use the French *déjà*, as the Lebanese do, but I like to use Arabic words in Arabic class.

I can easily convey the meaning without the word but I am a little stunned by the revelation. It's not surprising that some words in each of Arabic, French and English have no exact equivalent that I know of in the other two – the English 'bully'; the Arabic *ushq, samar* and *uns*; the French *or* and *dépaysé* – but they usually belong to a more specialised lexicon than everyday speech. How could my mother tongue fail to carry such a basic word?

# The War Is Over

A Saturday afternoon, 1979, not long before my seventeenth birthday. I am going to watch a movie with a friend, at the Salle Montaigne of the French Cultural Centre, a five-minute walk from my house in the neighbourhood of Mohammad el Hout, towards the Green Line. My friend is meeting me at the centre.

There has been an extended period of quiet in Beirut. Three years ago, the Syrian government of Hafez al-Assad sent its army into Lebanon to help its Christian militia allies, and prevent a coalition of Palestinian and Lebanese left-wing forces from prevailing in the war. The Druze leader of the coalition was assassinated shortly after, almost certainly by Syrian intelligence. But now, the Syrian government has fallen out with its erstwhile allies and Christian leaders are calling on Syrian occupation forces to withdraw from Lebanon. Though there has been no fighting of late, political tensions are high.

The French Cultural Centre is open, and this is a good sign. We Lebanese, desperate for optimism and always looking to resume our normal lives at the first opportunity, tend to ascribe too much significance to otherwise trivial pieces of information of this kind. 'If the French Cultural Centre has reopened and is staging public events', the logic runs, 'then surely things are fine'. Deep down, however, we know that these decisions – to open the centre to the public or not – are made by fallible individuals like ourselves, probably a Lebanese employee, rather than the French Intelligence Services, with as much ability to forecast the security weather as the average Beiruti, which is very little. But somehow, we continue to invest these announcements with far more significance than they deserve.

That the movie I am going to watch is Alain Resnais's *La guerre est finie* – The War Is Over – is accidental, if nicely ironic. Now, while my parents' apartment is firmly in West Beirut, the French Cultural Centre is located on Damascus Road, which for a long time has been the demarcation line

between East and West Beirut, a no-go area for civilians for much of the first phase of the civil war, between 1975 and 1977. But the roads have reopened, and people have been walking those streets again, even if residents haven't quite returned.

The French Cultural Centre has several buildings and two entrances, the main one on Damascus Road and a smaller side gate on Military Court Street, on the other side of the precinct. The latter has been open for public events: all the better, as it happens to be the side closer to my house and I can approach it on foot through quiet backstreets, without having to venture onto the actual Green Line, which retains something of a sinister aura. I am twenty metres away from the side entrance when I hear a yell from the first floor of the seemingly deserted and pockmarked building on the corner I have just turned.

'Stop! Raise your arms and don't move.'

I freeze and do as I am told. A few seconds later a Syrian soldier in full gear, machine gun at the ready, emerges from the building's entrance. Without saying a word, he raises a hand high above his head and slaps me on the face. My glasses fall on the ground, one of the lenses shattered.

He asks me what am I doing here. I mumble that I am going to the French Cultural Centre, pointing vaguely towards the entrance, which I now realise is deserted. He asks me what my name is and where I live. He tells me that this is a military area and I am not allowed here. We walk for a couple of minutes and enter a nondescript building only two streets away from my house.

The soldier delivers me to his officer, a middle-aged man sitting behind a desk, who asks me a few questions and explains that I have been arrested in a no-go zone. I am told to go home and to report back in a week. That I come from West Beirut and live next door, and that my name is Abbas, rather than George or Tony, must play in my favour.

I go home traumatised, and tell my family. What's most terrifying, I realise over the next few days, is that I am dealing with a foreign army, rather than the security organs of my own government, with no recourse to a legal process, and to which my family network of influence has no access.

When I go back to the military centre a week later, as instructed, my brother Jihaad, twelve years my senior, comes with me to help me deal with the Syrian soldiers. It's a mercifully brief affair. I report to the soldier at the entrance, explaining why I am here. He disappears for a minute and returns to say it's fine, we can go home, but I should never again venture where I was found, French Cultural Centre or not.

Though it may look like it, the war is not quite over, which a few months later proves to be spectacularly true, when fighting resumes with renewed vigour. And which, when I finally see *La guerre est finie*, turns out to be the predicament of the protagonist, played by Yves Montand: a left-wing veteran of the Spanish Civil War in whose psyche the war continues, long after he is exiled to Paris and General Franco consolidates his victory in Madrid.

# Sifr

It was Arabs who invented the number zero – *sifr*, with a strong s. A boast by our Arabic teachers that we find amusing. Yes, of course, Arabs invented 'nothing' – how typical! *Sifr* in Arabic means not only zero but also emptiness, void and nothingness.

In time, and as my high-school mathematics evolve, I come to appreciate how revolutionary is *sifr*: a number referring to that which doesn't exist. Counterintuitive, even a contradiction in terms, until a visionary invented it to demonstrate that it is not only possible but necessary. Without it, some branches of mathematics could not exist. That man is Mohammed al-Khawarizmi – a mathematician from Central Asia, working in Baghdad's House of Wisdom in the early ninth century – who also happened to invent algebra.

And then there are the aesthetics of *sifr*. It is written as a dot in the Indian numerals used by Arabs today – an apologetic symbol if ever there was one, trying to make itself as small as possible. Equally charming is *sifr* in Arabic numerals used by European languages – a little o, a gaping hole, offered by al-Khawarizmi himself, the absence of something rather than any positive presence. Both the dot and the hole are pleasantly hieroglyphic, with more than a touch of abstraction.

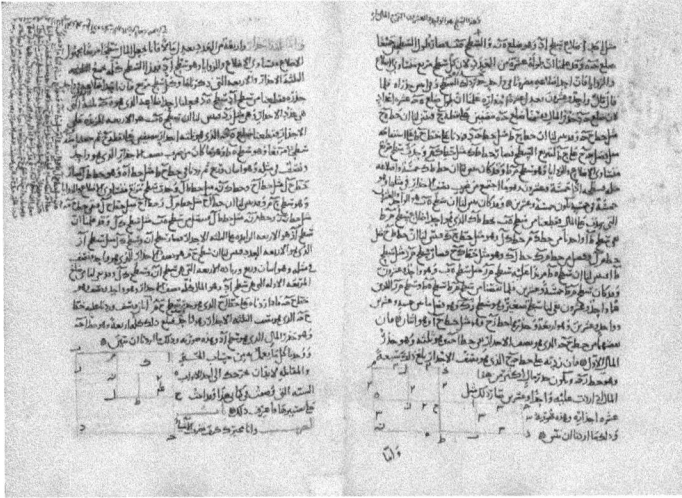

Excerpt from an al-Khawarizmi manuscript.

But what is most striking about *sifr* is its mysterious ability to oscillate between extremes. True, it has no impact on its sister numbers when added to them, a lesser integer ignored by its peers. But deploy it in multiplication and watch it devour any number it encounters, leaving no trace, turning it into another *sifr*, propagating through the world of digits like a virus, monstrously creating a world in its own image. *Sifr*, in other words, is the Jekyll and Hyde of numbers.

On the downside, it turns out that Arabs did not really invent zero. It was most likely the Indians who did so and, independently, the Mayans in south America, a few hundred years before al-Khawarizmi. The Arabs systematised its use from the eight century onwards, added it to their list of numbers and used it to invent algebra.

Which sounds better. We did not invent nothing; rather, we invented something out of nothing. Our Arabic teachers would surely approve of the new formulation.

# A Brief History of Mercy

Mr Raad is in the middle of a lesson on Arabic grammar. He writes on the whiteboard examples of composite *idafa*:

> (The) Garden (of the) Centre (of the) City
> (The) Hem (of the) Dress (of my) Mother

'And' he says, 'here is something familiar to you':

> (The) School (of) Lycée (of) Abdel Qader

Mr Raad pauses, as if he's having second thoughts, then turns around, now facing the class, one hand holding forth the chalk like a weapon, and the other one hovering by the waist, arm bent at the elbow, as if ready to pull an invisible gun from a non-existent holster. This is a typical Mr Raad posture, which is all the more peculiar since no man we know is more gentle or less military-looking than the always impeccably besuited Mr Raad.

'Do you know why your school is called Lycée Abdel Qader?' he asks. This is not the first time Mr Raad has digressed. Arms shoot up here and there. Most of us know the answer. Elementary, Monsieur Raad: it is because the West Beirut Street on which the school is located is called Rue Abdel Qader, hence Lycée Abdel Qader, to distinguish it from

Lycée Verdun, located in Rue Verdun, and Grand Lycée, in East Beirut's Ashrafieh, on the other side of the Green Line.

Mr Raad's avuncular bulk shifts in his teal-coloured, tight-fitting suit, his lips part a little and the edges of his generous moustache quiver, the hint of a smile forming.

'What I mean is, *who is* Abdel Qader, after whom the street is named?'

He might have added, 'you literal-minded twats', but Mr Raad is far too kind to be given to such putdowns. The class falls silent. Even the smart-arses and would-be-smart-arses – and I slot somewhere in between – are struck dumb.

Then two vertical arms appear, like solitary, long-dead stalks on parched land. Abdel Qader is the man who fought the French in Algeria in the nineteenth century, someone says. Correct, says Mr Raad, his smile now fully formed, his eyes twinkling.

'And do you know,' Mr Raad continues, 'that the illustrious emir Abdel Qader al-Jazairi once released his French prisoners of war rather than let them starve, because he was besieged by the French army and had barely enough food to feed his own soldiers?'

No, we didn't, we think in chorus, and good on him for doing so and what a fine man he must have been, but why are you telling us this, Mr Raad? Surely, this was a long, long time ago.

'And do you know what Napoleon did in Haifa, forty years earlier?' Mr Raad is obviously going somewhere with this – let's hope it's worthwhile. Not that we mind either way, as anything is better than grammar. Well, almost anything. We are now wise enough to assume that this last question is rhetorical. Even if it isn't, who would be brave enough to venture an answer? That Mr Raad has paused for a few seconds, giving us time to respond, is immaterial at best, a trap at worst.

'Napoleon besieged and captured 2,000 Turkish soldiers who were well stocked with food, while his own army was beginning to starve. He expropriated the food and ordered the prisoners killed because he wanted as much food as possible for his own soldiers and did not want to release his captives, lest they rejoin the enemy.

'And do you know what else he did, this overrated monster?' Mr Raad continues, no longer bothering to pause. 'He made sure the prisoners were executed by bayonets or by drowning, sometimes both, but not by shooting, because he did not want to "waste" ammunitions.'

Good on you, Mr Raad, and a thousand thank-yous for the story and its moral ammunition. *La guerre continue.* Can we stick it to Madame Vieillard now? Is the old crone as evil as the rest of them?

# Empire Strikes Back

Two of the most memorable *Alf Layla* stories of my childhood are *Alaa Dine wa'l Fanous Sihri* (Aladdin and the Magical Lamp) and *Ali Baba wa'l Arbaeen Harami* (Ali Baba and the Forty Thieves). They did not carry the same sexual charge as the frame story of Shahrazaad, but they were still as clever and entertaining as other *Alf Layla* tales. Open sesame – *iftah ya sumsum* – and the magic carpet might have become boring tropes for many, yet I still found the transformation of these two mundane household items into magical devices quite charming, and a sure sign of the genius of *Alf Layla*. It was quite a disappointment then when I first learnt that these two stories did not belong to the authentic *Alf Layla* and that it was the first French translator who had added them arbitrarily to the collection.

In 1704, Antoine Galland published the first translation of *Alf Layla* into a European language: French, in this case. To this day, Galland is credited with producing a translation of high literary worth and bringing *Alf Layla* to the world's attention. Dozens of translations into other European languages, including English, followed, and several Arabic manuscripts were subsequently discovered, while advances in printing technology from the early nineteenth century onwards brought the Arabic version to a wider audience.

*Alf Layla* arrived in Europe from Istanbul, Aleppo and Cairo at the beginning of the eighteenth century, during a steep rise in European power in the Mediterranean that would culminate in French and British colonisation of parts of North Africa and the Middle East in the next century. But the eighteenth and nineteenth centuries were also characterised by intense European interest in 'the Orient' – academic, political, diplomatic, popular – which, while producing valuable scholarship on Islamic and Arabic cultures, was often tainted by prejudice, poor science and lazy European notions of superiority.

Opening page of first volume of Antoine
Galland's translation of the 1001 Nights.

Orientalism, as this body of knowledge has come to be known, provided a scaffolding, ideological and instrumental, for the colonial subjugation of 'Orientals'. *Alf Layla*, a cause and an effect of increasing European fascination with the East, inevitably became part of this imperial history.

From the start, questions were raised about the authenticity of Galland's translation, and the liberties that he and subsequent translators took to make the tales more palatable to their audience. Galland, it turned out, omitted some stories from the Arabic manuscript he had access to, and borrowed others from other Arabic books and from stories told to him by a Syrian informant in Paris. Among the borrowed stories were two that would become most closely associated with *Alf Layla*: Aladdin and Ali Baba and the Forty Thieves.

The Arabic manuscript Galland used only contained around two hundred nights and, after the success of his first published volume, he was keen on completing the Thousand and One Nights – not knowing that the phrase was almost certainly an Arabic shorthand for a very large number, rather than a literal figure.

Another misunderstanding about *Alf Layla* was that, throughout its early history in Europe, it was seen by much of its readership as an actual depiction of life in the exotic East – a source of fascination and ridicule – rather than for what it was, an extraordinary body of literary fiction, partly of oral origins, written in the Arabic Middle Ages, about 500 years before the eighteenth century. Galland himself saw *Alf Layla* as an anthropological document of the contemporary Arab world, and his translation was explicitly marketed as a way of knowing it without having to travel there. In other words, Europe was doing to *Alf Layla* what it would do repeatedly in the colonised world: namely, taking possession of it, while misconstruing it through prejudice and self-interest.

The arrival of the tales in Europe, as today's scholars of *Alf Layla* concur, radically changed the book, and made it much harder to distinguish the original Arabic tales from their European incarnations. The late Harvard professor of Islamic philosophy Muhsin Mahdi showed that, in an ironic reversal, such was the fame of Galland's translation, it may well have influenced the choice of stories included in the first *Arabic* printed edition of the book, published in Cairo in 1826.

Mahdi, who was born and grew up in Iraq's southern city of Karbala, proposed in 1984 a thoroughly researched and carefully edited version of *Alf Layla*, now called the Leiden version, and based on a fourteenth-century manuscript, believed to be the earliest surviving one. The translation into English of Mahdi's version was completed by another Iraqi-born scholar, Hussain Haddawy, and published in 1990.

This symbolic reappropriation of *Alf Layla* by two Iraqi-born scholars, with their indigenous knowledge of the Arabic language – almost three hundred years after Galland acquired the manuscript from Aleppo, and interpreted it for Europe and the world – is itself a tale of empire striking back. Among its multiple ironies are that both Mahdi and Hadddawy partly trained in Western educational systems, further blurring any facile boundaries between East and West one might be tempted to draw. That the word 'empire' – which usually signifies imperial territories and institutions and/or those who run them – can also be taken to mean 'imperial subjects' further confounds any attempt to establish who exactly is 'striking back'.

European prejudice also left its mark on the portrayal of gender relations in *Alf Layla*, though not in the way one might expect. Strong-willed and powerful women appear frequently in original *Alf Layla* Arabic recensions. But European translations and recensions tended to suppress or diminish them, reflecting the conservatism of the male translators and the expectations of European readership in the eighteenth to early twentieth centuries. More recent feminist readings, and new translations and literary adaptations of the stories, have gone a long way towards restoring this dimension of *Alf Layla*.

Although the Mahdi-Haddawy version of *Alf Layla* is now considered the most historically authentic available to us, 'authenticity', when it comes to *Alf Layla*, is a slippery notion. The longer history of *Alf Layla* is one of multiple transformations of the text – from its oral sources, animated by *hakawaatis* and storytellers across cities of the Islamic East for hundreds of years, to its written forms, committed by scribes working away patiently, and sometimes creatively, in schools, libraries, the courts of sultans and in their own homes; from possible ancient Persian and Indian origins of the tales, through Abbasid accretions, adaptations, transformations and inventions in the ninth and tenth centuries, down to their incarnation in Mameluke times, in the fourteenth century; from the first European translations – Arabic to French, then from French to other European languages – to the multiple incarnations of *Alf Layla* today, including new recensions, new translations, essays, novels, stories, plays, even multiple Disney adaptations.

And, of course, my very own *Jeannie*, who has merged in memory with the image in my childhood picture book and continues to provide the most instinctive image I hold of Shahrazaad in mind. Was the artist who drew the image in my childhood picture book influenced by the maker of *Jeannie*? Or did the makers of the sitcom, on the other side of the globe, happen to see an English version of the same book I read in my childhood? Did they both draw inspiration from a third antecedent? Could that influence be the exquisite sketches found in Antoine Galland's book, propagating in time and space, through several centuries, right up to the present?

Or, more confusingly, is my memory playing tricks, remaking my picture book in the image of Jeannie? I can watch Jeannie today on Apple TV, but I have long since lost track of my picture book and hence have no way of answering these questions. And perhaps just as well, since this small personal conundrum of mine is charmingly emblematic of the larger history of *Alf Layla*.

# Lingua Franca

Growing up in multilingual Beirut – a few hours away from Europe, North Africa, the Arabian desert and the Indian subcontinent – I was immersed not only in several languages but in their politics, idiosyncrasies and hierarchies as well.

Lebanese was an unmistakably Arabic dialect that took words from French, English, Italian, Turkish and Persian, arabising their pronunciation and effortlessly adding them to its vocabulary. The most charming manifestation of this absorptive capacity could be found in the working-class lingo that gave us such gems as *ashakmen* (from the French *echappement*, for exhaust), *trunshkot* (for trench coat), *wa la doomare* (from the French *pas un demeurant*, meaning deserted). Or the Turkish *aywa* (yes), *oda* (room) and *gazuz* (fizzy drink). No self-respecting backgammon player would use Arabic numbers for the dice, but rather the musical Persian terms – *hab yek, shesh besh, doubara, banj w doo, doushash, dabash* – indissociable in a Lebanese mind from the sound of dice on the wooden board.

This openness to foreign languages was due in no small part to the fact that Lebanese was mostly a spoken dialect. It did not therefore face institutional barriers that written languages usually erect against adaptations from other languages. By contrast, the formal Arabic that we wrote was far less open to neologisms.

In the social world of middle-class Beirut, Arabic was seen as an archaic language, unable to engage with the modern world and its complexities. True, in many social circles, including that of my own parents, speaking good Arabic was a sign of authenticity, an antidote to the charge of colonial mimicry easily levelled against those Lebanese who used French in everyday life. But while an anti-colonial aptitude might earn you some admiration, it did not usually help you in job interviews or win you plaudits in high society.

I spoke Lebanese Arabic at home. Arabic was not only my mother tongue but the sole language that my mother spoke. Bookshelves in our house were filled with Arabic books, ancient and modern, and my eldest brother, father, grandfather and great-grandfather all wrote professionally in Arabic (as journalist, legal scholar, historian and religious cleric, respectively). Respect and appreciation for Arabic was instilled in me from an early age, a healthy counterweight to the disdain prevalent in the world outside my household.

In the Mission laïque française schools where I was educated, the ethos was as Gallic, secular and authoritarian as the name implied. In high school, science and math subjects were delivered only in French, sometimes by French teachers. But when it came to humanities and social sciences, we studied two curricula in parallel, one in French and one in Arabic: two sets of subjects for each of grammar, writing, literature, history and geography. Mercifully, the difference between the two sets of subjects was not just in the language of instruction: they also covered very different content.

Inevitably, our teenage minds engaged in a comparison of the two languages and Arabic did not usually fare well. The teaching of Arabic literature and grammar, in particular, was boring, unimaginative, often requiring rote learning. Arabic literature at school was either ancient poetry, whose concerns could hardly resonate with us – love-torn

Bedouins, feats of chivalrous knights, the stuff of courtly literature – or the modernist Lebanese texts of Gibran Khalil Gibran and Mikhail Neame, whose mix of spiritualism and Lebanese patriotism many of us found unappealing. Gibran and Neame, our rebellious teenage selves suspected, were second-rate writers sanctioned by the new Lebanese state because every nation needed its canon.

Against the material offered by our French literature teachers – the exquisite verses of Baudelaire, Rimbaud and Verlaine, the adventurous writing of Huysmans, or the gripping stories of Zola and Camus – Arabic literature, we came to believe, stood no chance. We had some inkling, but not much, of the murky colonial associations of some of the French writers we admired – the ambivalent settler politics of Albert Camus or Rimbaud's arms dealing in Abyssinia. The curriculum that my school followed mostly swept these uncomfortable truths under the table, in an unreconstructed take on history that I would later discover was characteristically French.

While we appreciated some of the Arabic poetry we were taught, a good proportion of the classical Arabic literature we were exposed to was written in a flowery style, with an excess of adjectives, adverbs and silly rhyming, which we found insufferable. By contrast, we duly admired the conciseness that our French-language, and later English-language, teachers taught us to appreciate.

As for science, it almost went without saying that for our impressionable minds Arabic was unsuitable for scientific communication, a conclusion we succeeded in reaching without reading a single scientific paper in our mother tongue.

Only much later would I begin to understand that ancient texts, whether in Arabic, French or English, had to be approached with a different sensibility and interpretative

Extract from Kamal al-Din al-Hasan ibn 'Ali ibn al-Hasan
al-Farisi, 'The Book of Correction of Optics for those who
have Sight and Mind'.

mind to more contemporary writing. What's more, there were plenty of far more interesting classical, as well as modern, Arabic texts that we had not been exposed to, some of which had been gathering dust on my family's bookshelves at home. That, in other words, I had attributed to Arabic literature a flaw of the conservative Arabic curriculum adopted by the Lebanese state and my own school.

And it would be several decades later, in Venice of all places, that I would come across an extract from the pioneering treatise on optics by Ibn al-Haytham, who was born in Basra in 965 and died in Cairo in 1040, in which he elaborates his theory of eyesight in Arabic, in one of the most disciplined, and altogether beautifully expounded scientific theories, I had ever come across.

I would discover that, rather than being prone to over-emphasis and protraction, or incapable of supporting rigorous, to-the-point writing of complex scientific ideas, Arabic had a striking conciseness intrinsic to it, in comparison with the two other languages I spoke fluently. But this I would have to find out for myself, long after I left school.

# Letters of the Sun and Letters of the Moon

There is a sweet economy of expression in Arabic, in its oral and written forms, and it comes about through a series of remarkable features, some less obvious than others, even to native speakers.

The definite article in Arabic is written as *al*. It is a soft word modifier attached to its beginning, rather than a word in its own right – the house is *albayt* and the airport is a*lmataar*. Nominative pronouns too are word modifiers – I, you, she, him, her, they, theirs – and so are some prepositions such as 'in', 'to' and 'as'. For example, the prefix for 'to' is *li* – 'to the house' is *lilbayt*, a formal contraction of *li-al-bayt*. 'To my house' and 'to her house' are *libayti* and *libaytiha*, the last syllable in each word indicating male or female pronouns. The five English words 'your shirt is like mine' are rendered in only two Arabic words – *qamisuka kaqamissi*. 'What is your name?' is *Maa ismuki?* and 'Where are you going?' is *Ayna tathaab?*

Now, *al* is gender neutral and is always written thus. But the l is sometimes silent. This depends on whether the letter that comes immediately after it is lunar (*qamarya*) or solar (*shamsya*). We say al*forn* for the bakery but a*ssayara* for the car (instead of al*sayara*), because the Arabic letter f is *qamarya*, while the letter s is *shamsya*. Whenever the first letter that comes after 'al' is *shamsya*, the l becomes silent, in a tiny phonetic contraction.

Half of the twenty-eight letters of the Arabic alphabet are solar and the other half lunar, in this delightful celestial metaphor. Unless they are linguists, native Arabic speakers like myself usually know which is which by sound, rather than memory: that is, they are able to tell by trying out the letter – saying *alsayara* or *afforn* sounds wrong to their ear.

Words in Arabic also tend to have a smaller number of letters because short vowels in Arabic are not letters, but rather signs added to a skeleton of consonants that makes up the word. For example, the word *th-h-b* means either 'he went' (pronounced 'tha-ha-ba' and written *thhb*, the accents indicating the a) or 'gold' (pronounced 'tha-ha-b' and written *thhb*). School-educated native Arabic speakers learn from an early age to read without a need to see the vowels, inferring pronunciation and meaning from context. Hence, books, newspapers and handwriting almost never show the short vowels. That the language can only be written cursively, and that Arabic calligraphic traditions have evolved ever denser scripts, lends a compactness to the written form that echoes its spoken counterpart.

Another source of conciseness is that the words 'am' and 'have' do not exist in Arabic, at least not in the same way as in European languages such as English or French, because the grammatical structure of the language makes them redundant. Arabic grammar distinguishes between verbal and nominal sentences. The former are conventional sentences, structured with verbs, subjects and objects, but usually involving some action, something being done. The word for verb in Arabic literally means 'act of doing', a subject is a 'doer' and an object a 'done-to'.

On the other hand, whenever a sentence revolves around some form of 'being' or 'having', no verb is required because, following the same logic, there is no 'doing' involved. Therefore, there is no need for 'am' and 'have'. These 'noun sentences' (*joumla ismia*) have a simpler, shorter grammatical structure. This explains why you might hear Arabic native speakers say, upon first learning English, 'I hungry' – odd in English, but it makes sense in Arabic.

The overall effect of these features working together is remarkable. An expression such as 'In the name of God, the merciful, the compassionate' requires nine words in English but only four in Arabic (*Bismil-lah arrahman arrahim*) and sounds even shorter because the first two words are pronounced as though they are joined together ('bismillah') through a formal construction called *idafa*. In addition, r, the first letter of *rahman* and *raheem*, is solar, gifting the speaker this extra little syllabic contraction.

The Quran's Fatiha chapter – the most widely recited by Muslims around the world, and often the first to be taught to children – is made up of 32 Arabic words, typically rendered in around 70 English or French words by professional translators.

But this density arguably reaches its spectacular best in *Alf Layla*. In the Bulaq version, dating to 1826, page after page of unrelenting stories are conveyed by cursive, mostly unpunctuated fonts, with no short vowels shown and words seeming almost to run into each other, in a form reminiscent of shorthand:

فلما كانت الليلة العاشرة

A page from the 10th night of the 1001 Nights,
Arabic Bulaq version, 1826.

it cme to m o hpp kng tht thr ws a fshrm nd he ws old nd
he hd a wfe nd thr chldrn nd he ws poor nd dsprte to feed
thm nd he thrw hs net into the sea one lst tme hs prvs thr
ttmpts on tht dy hd lft hm wth heavy hrt yldng aftr much
hvng pshng nd pllng the crcss of an ass a drm of soil drt nd
a bndl of brkn rthnwre this frth tme smthng heavy cght in
his net agn nd the fshrmn grd hmslf for nthr dsppntmnt ...

The page can be difficult to decipher for students of Arabic. But for the native or trained Arabic speaker, the brevity of the writing is no obstacle to fluency of reading. Quite the contrary: this remarkable conciseness feeds into a relentless narrative pace, as the tales progress without hindrance, carrying the breathless reader with them.

Only Shahrazaad's recurrent appearance, at the end of each night – '[b]ut morning overtook Shahrazad, and she lapsed into silence' – gives the reader brief respite, allowing both to take a breath of fresh air, before diving in again with addictive pleasure.

# A Pair of Shorts

I walk into a clothes store in Hamra to buy a pair of shorts. I see Mona at the far corner of the women's section on the ground floor, holding a shirt against her chest and looking at herself in a mirror. I head straight towards her and say hi. She has a beautiful smile and sparkling eyes behind her lenses, still as sweet as that first day in *sixième*. We're studying at different universities and haven't come across each other for a few years now. We have quite a bit of catching up to do. We make a joke about *class sixième* and how young and gullible and hopelessly bespectacled we were. Fifteen minutes later we say goodbye to each other. She goes back to her shirt. I walk out of the shop, into Jeanne d'Arc street, and as I reach the university campus, five minutes later, I realise that I have forgotten to buy my pair of shorts.

# Refracted Grief

My maternal grandmother, Um Abdel Ameer, is in her late fifties and lives alone in her house in the village of Sh'hoor, a few kilometres to the east of Tyre. In March 1978, news starts spreading of an impending invasion by the Israeli army. Soon, Israeli warplanes start dropping, in addition to bombs, leaflets poorly written in Arabic, asking the population to leave and warning villagers not to harbour *mukharribeen*. This archaic Arabic word means 'people who break things', literally 'saboteurs'. But it is more suited to chiding a mischievous child than describing soldiers engaged in sabotage. The word *irhaabi* – 'terrorist' – has not yet gained currency.

As the bombardments intensify and panic mounts in the village, my grandmother decides to leave. She packs a small suitcase, gets into a taxi with two relatives of hers, a young woman in her thirties and her teenage daughter, and they head for the safety of Beirut. My grandmother sometimes comes for visits to the city anyway and stays with us. But two days after leaving Sh'hoor, the car and its occupants have still not arrived at their destination, with conflicting rumours circulating about their whereabouts.

My mother is a nervous wreck while waiting for news, and it is as painful to watch her as it is to think of my grandmother trapped in a war zone. Last time my grandmother stayed with us, a few weeks earlier, she left in a huff, upset by something my mother had said to her. Now, my mother is tormented by guilt at not having tried to make up with her.

She goes over everything that can conceivably go wrong. What if she's trapped somewhere? What if she's forgotten her tablets? What if she has been shot by the Israelis? What if she's been kidnapped and raped? My mother has always had a knack for voicing the darkest thoughts we might collectively be harbouring, a master at stoking fears. Trying to reassure her is self-defeating, because all it does is make her double down. She is now acting as if the worst fate has already befallen my grandmother. My father's temperament is the diametrical opposite: always an optimist, sometimes to the point of self-delusion. Watching the two of them argue can be highly entertaining, if not for the fact that on this occasion the subject matter is so morbid.

We are all relying on my uncle Abdel Ameer, who lives in Tyre. He gets into his car and scours the south looking for his mother, despite the still-raging war. He quizzes relatives and taxi drivers, and enquires in hospitals and health centres. At last, a week or so later, he finds her and her fellow passengers under the rubble of a house in the village of Abbassyeh, not far from Sh'hoor. Her body is so mangled it is unrecognisable, and he is only able to identify her from the clothes she is wearing. My uncle does what he can to gather her remains, and that of her companions, and have them buried in the local cemetery.

From accounts of villagers in Abbassyeh, he reconstructs the final moments of the doomed travellers. As the taxi was passing through the village, bombing intensified, the driver stopped the car, and everyone got out and ran for cover, as fast as they could. My grandmother was injured while running and had to be carried to the nearest house which, a few moments later, was destroyed by Israeli warplanes. Not far from the house and not long after, a mosque where more than a hundred civilians were sheltering was flattened.

Upon hearing the news in Beirut, my mother shrieks with pain, then falls silent for days. When my paternal uncle was killed, six years earlier, there was a surreal quality to the event, as if I was being initiated into something more extraordinary than tragic. My grandmother's death is different, not least because my mother's grief is so pervasive that it becomes the medium through which I experience the aftermath.

I watch her, a week later, sitting quietly among the mourners in our living room, slumped small in the corner of a three-seated sofa, in a black dress, a white shawl pulled back halfway over her hair, her face dry and sullen. I have the distinct feeling that, in the days prior to receiving confirmation of her mother's death, even she did not really believe her own premonitions. That, through the logic of an anguished mind, the thoughts she was airing were little more than an attempt at forcing the world to give her back her mother, safe and sound. By bringing to the fore the worst possible outcomes, she had hoped to have them dismissed, bending reality to her will, as it were, making it snap back into a less terrifying shape. And that, in the maelstrom of guilt and grief now raging quietly in her mind, part of her believes that her own dark thoughts may have spilled into reality instead, and have hastened its unfolding along the bleakest possible pathway.

# Barbarians at the Gate

From 1978 onwards, wars, near and far, erupt with alarming frequency in the wider Middle East. In January of that year, the Shah of Iran leaves the country after months of widespread protests and, two weeks later, Ayatollah Khomeini returns from his exile. In time, Khomeini's supporters, by far the most powerful elements among the revolutionaries, prevail. The new Islamist government bans and sometimes physically eliminates its left-wing and liberal rivals, paving the way for a Shia theocracy in Tehran.

In December 1979, the Soviet army invades Afghanistan to prop up the regime of Babrak Karmal against his centrist rivals, expecting quick victory. The Islamic Mujahideen, supported by American and Saudi weapons, have other ideas and engage the invaders in guerrilla warfare in the rugged terrain of the Afghan countryside. Less than ten years later, in February 1989, the Soviet government completes the withdrawal of its troops, all but admitting defeat. The Soviet Union itself collapses soon after. In Afghanistan, civil war follows the Soviet withdrawal, until 1996, when the Taliban finally march into Kabul and take power.

On 22 September 1980, Saddam Hussein, an ally of the United States, orders his army to invade Iran, launching a bloody war, during which he uses chemical weapons against civilian populations and both sides engage in extensive bombing of major urban centres. Eight years and half a million dead later, the two countries, exhausted by the human and economic cost of the war, agree to cease hostilities and return to pre-war borders. Hussein, smarting from the financial toll of the war, invades his southern neighbour and erstwhile ally Kuwait in August 1990, in order to seize its lucrative oil fields, but he is expelled within a few weeks by a coalition of Western powers headed by the United States.

In March 1978, Menahem Begin, another ally of the United States, orders the Israeli army to invade south Lebanon. Palestinian guerrillas – mostly refugees from the 1948 war intent on liberating their homeland – have been staging attacks across the border from Lebanon. The Israeli government wants to pacify the border by creating a buffer zone inside Lebanese territory. Begin's party, the Likud, had come to power nine months earlier pushing a hardline agenda. Four years later, on 6 June 1982, the Israeli government ups the ante by ordering a wholesale invasion of its northern neighbour, which leaves in its wake extensive destruction and hundreds of thousands dead, injured and displaced. Most of the fatalities are Lebanese and Palestinian civilians but hundreds of Israeli soldiers also die. The operation succeeds in expelling the PLO from Beirut to Tunis, more than 2,000 kilometres across the Mediterranean from the Israeli capital.

This time the Israeli government wants nothing less than a peace treaty with a new Lebanese client state. But the Israeli order comes crumbling down over the following months, amid violence and bloodshed, and the treaty lasts less than ten months, with the Lebanese parliament revoking it in March 1984.

Meanwhile, on 9 December 1987, an intifada breaks out in Gaza, then spreads to the West Bank, in protest at Israeli occupation. The Israeli army responds with shocking brutality – firing live rounds at protesters, beating teenagers with clubs and rocks, demolishing houses, deporting activists, and incarcerating tens of thousands of Palestinians. The intifada lasts until 1991, when the US-sponsored Madrid peace conference is launched. All in all, more than a thousand Palestinians and 150 Israelis are killed during the intifada. Two years later, the Oslo Accords are signed, which see the PLO moving from Tunis to Ramallah in the West Bank, less than forty-five kilometres from Tel Aviv.

# West Hall

February 1984. Shia militiamen have overrun West Beirut, expelling the Lebanese army under President Ameen Gemayel. Now that the fighting is over, they gather boisterously on street corners, in post-battle fatigue, with weapons slung casually on their shoulders. Their swagger is full of self-righteous revolutionary zeal, newfound Islamic piety – made mostly in Lebanon but also inspired by the Iranian revolution – and a good dose of class resentment. Ras Beirut bears the brunt. This is the 'bohemian' district of the city, where AUB – the American University of Beirut – is located. But this is a particular kind of bohemian, Lebanese-style, one which rarely breaks with its class roots – mostly an experimental, self-questioning phase that Lebanese youth from middle-class, well-to-do families go through before they 'grow up' and move overseas to pursue wealth or education, often both.

The Shia eruption brings us together, the would-be-bohemians, more than ever. We make a point of drinking beer more conspicuously on West Hall – the campus focal point, where much of student life takes place – to the disapproving looks of piously bearded students.

One professor becomes a legend as it emerges that, when harassed by a militiaman on the corner of Abdel Aziz and Bliss streets – outside the campus but only twenty metres from its eastern entry point, the Medical Gate – he gave his tormentor a mighty slap on the face before bolting onto the campus. The hapless militiaman was stopped from pursuing him by the campus guards.

Beirut is ours, not yours, we are saying collectively. Good on you for helping to scupper the humiliating 'peace' agreement between Israel and Lebanon but, around here, don't you dare tell us what to do and how to be. And don't lecture us on anti-colonialism and nationalism – this campus has been fertile ground for the Lebanese and Palestinian progressive left over the past fifty years, and we consider ourselves heirs to this proud tradition.

The harassment lasts a few months, after which the militiamen let it go. Following an accelerated version of Ibn Khaldun's theory, and a time-honoured Lebanese tradition, the hardened warriors, with their half-baked moral policing, grudgingly accept the decadent ways of the city – and sometimes, even better, join in with them wholeheartedly.

The West Hall at the American University of Beirut (copyrights American University of Beirut).

# Bodies on the Line

Sunday afternoon, spring of 1985. My girlfriend, Haala, and I hear the roar of two motor vehicles, likely to be vans or pick-up trucks, in an otherwise quiet street. They pull over and leave their engines running. We are alone in an apartment on the ground floor of a charming four-storey building in the Ras Beirut neighbourhood.

A commotion follows, and we hear several people – men, women and children – speaking in an easily recognisable southern-Lebanese accent. There is also the distinctive clatter of dense metal, which we recognise as the unlatching of the barrier at the back of a truck and, we suspect, one or two machine guns being passed around.

When the banging on the door of our apartment starts, our fear is confirmed: the visitors are here for us. Haala and I keep still. All our windows are shuttered and, if we make no noise, we reason, they have no way of knowing there is anyone inside. Hopefully, they will go away. The silence is heavy in between bouts of frantic door-knocking – the motor engines have now been switched off.

'Try again,' we hear one of the men saying outside a window. 'They are usually here.'

They do, twice more, while our hearts are racing. We hear the murmur of further consultation, which we cannot make out except for the word *lamirkieh* – the American woman – after which we hear footsteps and, a few moments later, the sound of trucks driving away.

I peek through the slits of the wooden shutters to confirm that they have left, go to the kitchen and return with two mugs of hot chocolate. Haala and I snuggle under the blankets and exchange a few jokes. Where would we hide if our visitors force the door? Consensus is inside the two gigantic vases in the living room: our heads would stick out, so we would have to freeze to perfection, but at least we could communicate with each other with nods and winks throughout the ordeal. Which kitchen implements would we use to fight back? I offer the frying pan, suggesting we could whack a few militiamen on the head, then run out the door into the street as fast we can. Haala dismisses my idea as unimaginative, insisting instead on a plastic spatula she would gladly stick in the leader's neck, pinning him to the wall until he yields to our demands.

We are immensely relieved, and not a little pleased with ourselves for outwitting the militiamen. But, as we have suspected, this isn't the end of the story. Our less-than-charming visitors will come back, a few days later, more determined to get what they want this time around.

Haala and I lived with our respective parents and depended for privacy on the occasional borrowed apartment from friends of friends. Holding hands on a secluded bench on campus or kissing in the darkness of a cinema, though easily achievable, was not quite so satisfying. My family apartment was rarely empty and hers was out of bounds for me, what with her strict father.

The four years of my undergraduate studies coincided with a period of political upheaval and violence in Beirut. Typically, an event would trigger a bout of fighting for a few days or a couple of weeks; classes would be suspended, then resume as soon as it was over. The pace could be relentless, but it was possible to continue to live with a semblance of normality. The Biblical inscription on the small, charming clocktower adorning the main gate of AUB – "That They May Have Life and Have it More Abundantly" – was an apt description of our lives in those days, although not in the way those who chose the quote would have anticipated. (The Tower Clock itself would be destroyed by a car bomb in November 1991, before being rebuilt.) On the other hand, a gradual breakdown of law and order after 1984 meant that Shia and Druze militias now ran West Beirut, the part of the city in which Haala and I lived.

I am in a car with a friend of mine, having just dropped off Haala around midnight. We are waiting for her to wave at us from her balcony and confirm that she has reached home safely. The routine is only necessary because we have to drop her off twenty metres or so down the street from her building, lest her father sees us, then park somewhere discreet within view of her balcony.

While we are waiting, two men from the Shia militia Amal appear out of nowhere, guns in hand, knock on the driver's window and ask us to get out of the car. Two young men sitting quietly in a car close to midnight is not a good look, especially when there have been sporadic attacks by a Sunni militia against Amal and, though I was a Shia, my friend was a Sunni. We do not want to tell them the real reason for hanging around, to spare Haala neighbourhood gossip. As we cannot provide a plausible explanation for our lurking, the militiamen insist that we should come with them to the nearest detention centre.

'We just want to ask you a few questions.'

Which means, at best, some rough treatment, a black eye or a slap on the face, and a few hours in a dark room until someone makes a call to the militia leader on our behalf; or, at worst, a few days of detention and God knows what else. I refuse to comply and say to the men that we have done nothing wrong, that we are university students who live in West Beirut and there is no reason for them to take us away.

Upon which, one of the militiamen points his gun at my groin and shoots, but only after tilting it down at the last instant, aiming at a point between my feet. This is a new line of argument that, needless to say, I find persuasive.

Just as we are about to comply, we see Haala sprinting down the street, waving her arms and yelling. She tells the militiamen, while catching her breath, that we are her friends – she is a local; they know her. She has heard us arguing with them, has thrown caution to the wind and has come to our rescue, our brave and beautiful knight-in-a-frock. Hearing the gunshot on her way has alarmed her, but her timing is perfect. They let us go, though not without making a snide remark to Haala.

It was hardly surprising, then, that we always jumped at any opportunity for an empty flat, a weekend here or an overnight there. Such opportunities arose because, after the Israeli invasion and the destruction wrought in 1982, a large number of refugees from south Lebanon were still living in camps in and around Greater Beirut. When an apartment was deemed unoccupied, even just for a few days, militiamen from Amal would force it open and bring in a refugee family. There was a rough kind of justice in this housing practice, with impoverished men and women, displaced from rural south Lebanon, using their newfound power to take on the affluent city that often looked down on them. But it had generated fear among Beirutis, and anyone planning to leave their house, whether for days or years, had to make sure house-sitting was arranged at all times.

When a family friend asked me whether I would be willing to move into the apartment of a friend of hers for two weeks, I said yes. The apartment's owner was an American woman in her sixties who was going on a visit to the United States. She had family roots in the Levant and had been living in Beirut for many years. That she was American made the apartment more vulnerable to a takeover, and my Shia background, the oppressor's creed, probably made me more attractive to her as a temporary occupant. For Haala and me, it was a God-sent holiday where we could have all the privacy we wanted.

I met with my host a few days before she was due to leave. She showed me around the apartment, asked me to feel at home and thanked me for my willingness to house-sit. I promised to look after the apartment, and moved in on the day she left. Haala and I purchased wine, meat and a collection of our favourite cheeses. We brought a selection of our favourite cassettes and records. We were very much looking forward to this little break, the first time we had shared an apartment for more than a day or two.

Meanwhile, across the street was a man who spent much of his time bare-chested on the roof of his one-storey house, with no useful occupation other than watching the comings and goings in the neighbourhood. It didn't take him long to notice the absence of the American woman, and see the apartment's new occupants coming and going. The man, we would find out later, was a squatter who had contacts with the militias.

They choose their timing better the second time. They arrive at night and the lights are on in the apartment, visible from the street. As soon as I open the door, the men stride in, guns in hand, and the women and children soon follow with their belongings. Nasty words are uttered, including *jawaasees*, 'spies', and *beit daara*, 'whorehouse' – either of which is a serious accusation in the current atmosphere in the city, let alone both. The words are probably meant to bully us and need not be taken seriously – but you can never be certain.

Haala isn't here on this occasion and, as it happens, what the militiamen see when they walk in, rather than the women-in-negligées or the CIA cell they might have expected, are three young men sitting at a table, surrounded by piles of thick engineering books and a profusion of handwritten mathematical equations. It is examination period, and we are studying in earnest. We must have cut rather nerdy figures.

I argue with the militiamen, telling them again and again that the apartment is already occupied, thank you very much, and that the owner, who's been living here for decades, will be back in a few days. Another friend of mine drops in by chance, and then my sister Hiam arrives and enters the fray. Never one for mincing words, she gives the militiamen a piece of her mind; fortunately, gender dynamics mean that she is more likely to get away with it than a man, and the militiaman at the receiving end of her tongue-lashing takes it silently.

At some point in the affair, we seem to have reached a surreal standstill, with my friends and I sitting around the table, refusing to budge, staring at each other, while the refugee families are moving in and making themselves at home all around us. That my three friends and class buddies are sticking with me, rather than making a dash for it, is all the more heroic, as one is a Greek Orthodox Christian and the other two are Sunni, denominations that put them at a distinct disadvantage in volatile, Shia-dominated Beirut.

My insistence on staying is not without negotiating value, because the refugee women would be loath to share a house with a strange man. On the other hand, my advantage is fragile and would vanish if the militiamen decide to expel us from the house by force. So far, they have not used or even threatened physical violence, and I am playing it by ear. Negotiating with gun-wielding men is an art that all Beirutis have practised at some point in the fifteen-year war – deciding, based on the specific situation and the stakes involved, whether there is room for reasoning or whether to give in to save oneself from further indignities or worse.

Besides, my trump card is being played elsewhere. The office of the militia leader Nabih Berri – warlord of the hour, ally of the Syrians and future parliamentary-speaker-cum-corrupt-politician – has been contacted, in the hope that he might instruct his men to leave us alone.

But it is my friends and I who eventually walk away on that night. We do so after receiving assurances from the militia leader's office that when the American woman returns, the refugees will vacate, but my friends and I have to leave first.

As it happens, the refugees do vacate but only a few days after the woman comes back, and not without causing some damage to the apartment. She has had to share her home with strangers for those few days, but at least she has got it back. When I see her, after the refugees have left, I hear nothing but gratitude from her and she seems to have no ill feelings towards the refugees.

As for Haala and I, our little holiday-in-war is over before we know it, and we are soon back to the fragile but sweet safety of dark movie theatres. A few weeks after the apartment incident, we go to Cinema Clemenceau, which has only just reopened after a bout of fighting; most Beirutis are still reluctant to leave their homes. The projectionist-cum-ticket-seller-cum-usher is sitting on a chair in the lobby, smoking. He is a hefty lad, balding, with a thick moustache and fleshy lips. He tells us we are the only customers so far and, unless more turn up, he will not run the session.

It's a no-brainer: Haala and I pay for an extra ticket, walk into the theatre and try a few different seats – some are less ragged, more upholstered than others – before choosing our spot. As we walk away from the cinema two hours later, hand in hand, with the nocturnal silence of deserted streets hanging over us like a pergola on a summer day, there is, we decide, something to be said for wars after all.

# Can the Subaltern Run?

There is in the history of the disempowered an undercurrent of fight and run, of run and fight. The pivotal turning moment between the two acts is a form of wisdom. The subaltern may or may not be able to speak but they will always be quick on their feet.

# THREE:
# THE REALITY PRINCIPLE

# Window Seat

On 23 September 1986, aged twenty-three, I boarded a Middle East Airlines plane from Beirut to London Heathrow. I had bid farewell to a few close friends at the Sporting Beach Club on the day before my departure, and to most of my family at the doorstep of our house just before getting into the car taking me to the airport. I'd been on short visits to London twice as a teenager, but on this occasion, I was leaving Lebanon to do my postgraduate studies in the United Kingdom and so was going to live overseas for a few years, for the first time in my life.

Ensconced in a window seat and armed with the colourful map of the inflight magazine, including a two-page foldout across which a curved arrow bridged Beirut to London, I could trace the plane's trajectory from the sun-drenched south-east shore of the Mediterranean to the north-west of Europe and the British Isles.

The sky was mostly clear, and I had an excellent view of the seascape we were flying over, the only blemish on the scenery caused by the scratches on the double-glazed plastic window. The first two hours of the six-hour flight were over the vast scintillating body of water: breathtaking, a little terrifying, but in strangely familiar shades of blue, with squiggly coastlines and rocky outcrops. When the aeroplane reached the Greek archipelago, it swerved sharply north-west, cruising over Central Europe and France, then on to the English Channel.

As the plane approached London, it sliced through a thick layer of cloud, turbulence shaking the aircraft violently, as if I was crossing a threshold, leaving behind one kind of reality and entering another one. The plane's wings finally steadied, the fog thinned out and London's suburbia shimmered into view – deep-green meadows, overcast sky, gravity-defying drops of rain running up my window, and those famous rows of identical red-brick houses which, in time, flying back and forth between London and Beirut, would come to evoke for me a dreariness like no other.

I was excited and apprehensive, sensing that I was parting with something visceral in myself, with no return option. The strange thing was that, over the next few weeks, as homesickness rose in me and abated, my mind went over that watershed trip from Beirut again and again and, as it did so, it kept foregrounding as a moment of separation not, as I had expected, the take-off from Beirut airport or the emotional farewells prior, but the moment in time when my plane left the Ionian Mediterranean behind and headed further north, landwards.

This was news to me. Thus far, like most Beirutis, I had held in my mind various identities at various times – Lebanese, Arab, Shia, Levantine, Beiruti, atheist, cultural Muslim, leftist, Southern Lebanese, Lycéen – but none were associated with a body of water. I had not, that is, thought of myself as Mediterranean.

# Greetings from Southampton

Six months after my arrival in England, I learn that someone showing me the sole of their shoes is not a mark of
disrespect and I can relax. I also find out that, in England,
joining all five fingertips of one hand, pointing up, and
shaking them up and down at someone – a common gesture
in Lebanon – is not understood as intended, namely, 'slow
down'. This I discover when a man who is driving a little too
fast towards the pedestrian crossing that I am about to stride
onto responds to my gesture by sticking his tattooed arm
out of the car window and giving me the all-too-universal
two fingers.

But my most memorable lesson in cross-cultural misunderstanding comes when I walk into the main office of the
department of civil engineering of the University of
Southampton, where I am studying for my master's degree.
I want to speak to the secretary about something and notice
that Howard Allen, a reserved professor who teaches us
structural stability and whom I have seen twice in the
corridor earlier that day, is standing at the other end of the
room. When he sees me, he exchanges a brief look with the
secretary, then raises his head and turns towards me: 'I said
hello to you three times today: is this enough?'

I am mortified. It turns out that, unbeknownst to me, I am
the terror of the school corridor, because I have a tendency

to say hello to people I know every time I cross paths with them, even if it means saying it multiple times to the same person on the same day. It is instinctive, unpremeditated.

What makes it worse is that I sometimes say, 'How are you?' instead of 'Hello'. This is because, in Arabic, a common form of greeting is *keefak*, which means 'How are you?' – even if the greeter usually expects a monosyllabic answer or a nod in return, rather than an actual conversation.

Another bodily habit bites the dust.

# Bina

I am woken up by a knock on the door of my room at Montefiore House, the university hall of residence in Southampton. An acquaintance of mine, a Greek student, is at the door, her boyfriend by her side, and she's crying. Bina, a mutual friend who also lives at Montefiore House, died last night. She was walking back from uni when she was run over by a car as she tried to cross the street. It was a rainy night, visibility was poor, and it appears that Bina did not see the oncoming vehicle when she decided to cross.

Bina and I have become close over the past few weeks. We were not dating, not yet, but that's where I think we were heading. She was from an Indian background, though she was born and spent the first few years of her life in Kampala before Idi Amin expelled Indians from Uganda.

I go with another two friends to the mortuary to see her one last time. Her parents travel from the North of England for the memorial ceremony in Southampton. A few weeks later, I rent a flat in the city and move out of Montefiore House for good.

# Doctorhood

The PhD graduation ceremony is on today at the University of Southampton. True, I am rather bored with engineering, but I have a challenging, well-paid, travel-frequent job in the picturesque south of England, in the heart of the New Forest, where I spend my time writing exquisite mathematical equations and turning them into computer programs that engineers at Honda R&D in Tokyo use in designing their engines.

Glamorous as the job may sound in the world of engineering, and much as I continue to enjoy working with mathematics, the rarefied world of simulation in which I dwell for most of the day is becoming deeply unsatisfying. The ship I would rather be on – writing – has sailed a long time ago, for all I know. I have moved out of university accommodation and live in a rented apartment in Southampton, a city of real-estate agents and manicured lawns, which doesn't seem to offer much outside university life, at least not to foreigners like me.

I can still muster excitement at my imminent graduation and am sufficiently cynical to subscribe to the medieval ritual. And, in any case, formally finishing my studies is cause for celebration. Several friends of mine will be celebrating with me today – though no family – and that is something to look forward to. Nor is it above me to take pleasure in the thick, leather-bound degree document, the likes of which I still remember fondly from my bachelor's degree graduation, four years ago in Beirut.

The handful of other PhDs-to-be and I are appropriately dressed – hood, gown and shiny shoes – and seated in alphabetical order at the front of the hall, markedly separate from the undergraduate graduates, ready for the ceremonial culmination of three years of ardent study, poor diet and countless games of snooker.

My name is finally called out. I walk up the side steps with as much aristocratic mien as I can possibly muster, towards the chancellor of the university, who is waiting for me, centre stage, with a smile. I was told, just before the ceremony started, that no documents would exchange hands, and that the actual degree would be posted to me later on. I reach the chancellor, who clasps my right hand with both of his and whispers in my ear, asking what am I doing next. I have five milliseconds to answer him, which is more than I need. I mumble something eminently forgettable before we both turn to face the camera. Then I step away, walking towards the other side of the stage, down the stairs, relieved and empty-handed.

# Beaulieu

I am nipping out from my office in the New Forest to buy
lunch. It's a five-minute drive to the nearest village, Beaulieu.
I ask Jane if she would like anything from the shops. Jane is
a secretary who has become a friend.

'Where are you going?' she asks.

'Bo'l'eu,' I say, using the French pronunciation of this
unmistakably French name.

She stares at me blankly.

'B'you'liou', I repeat, trying the word's English pronunciation,
the bitter taste of French-language blood on my tongue.

Jane smiles at my funny accent.

Miss Spear was one thing, three hours per week at most in
high school, a little exotic diversion, quickly forgotten. This
is something else: I now live among the word-butchers.

# English Mysteries

I am intrigued by English. On the plus side, there is a sense of unending discovery. New words. New ways of saying things. New concepts and new shades of meaning. I start writing stories about the civil war in Lebanon in English and there is something refreshing about exploring my youthful experiences through the lens of another language.

Among its many virtues is its not being French. A colonial language, true, but not *my* colonisers. The British monarchy did not lord it over us Lebanese. I did not go to an English school, had no English school principals to contend with, and no unreconstructed imperial English history was foisted on me.

Some English words I use in my stories help me to see aspects of my experience that I haven't seen before or haven't had the means to articulate. Words for the human anatomy, for one. The *midriff* and the *small of one's back* and the *cheekbones*. The *cuticle* and the *purlicue* and the *earlobe*. Equivalent words in classical Arabic almost certainly exist but mostly they languish in old books, never making it into our day-to-day Lebanese. And there are all the playful-sounding nouns and adjectives. *Dumbfounded* and *flabbergasted* and *razzamatazz*. Sometimes I channel my stories in a way designed to help me use a new word I like. Remarkably easy, especially because for now I am not too worried about plot and character and narrative structure. What matters more is experimenting with words, like a child playing with a toy that keeps on giving. I am surprised by the strange pleasure I get out of this.

Other English words, though, seem to come up short. They transform the experience that I am trying to describe but not in a good way. What I perceive when I reread what I have written is not what I have in mind, not when I compare it to its equivalent Arabic expression, and I seem to have no alternative. A 'roadblock' is not quite what *hajiz* conveys. 'Party' and 'gathering' are no match for the sensual conviviality of *sahra* and *sahar*; neither do 'place' (or the Italian import 'piazza') and 'surface' come close to the richness of *saaha* and *massaaha*. 'Uncle' is far too bland, and a touch too avuncular, next to *aam* and *khaal*, two words that carry shades of kinship and loyalty, and hints of power struggles and family feuds.

Meanings and connotations are lost while others are gained, but words are not fungible and there is no calculus of costs and benefits to be had in language. Each sentence must earn its place in the world on its own merit, and one is left to mourn the losses while enjoying the gains.

# Keef Mazejak

The word *keef* is the adverb 'how' – as in *keefak*, for 'How are you?' – from the formal Arabic *kayf*. But *kayf* also means a state of exaltation or exhilaration: *ala kayfak* means 'as you like it', as does the Levantine *ala mazejak*, from *mazej* for 'mood' and *mazeje* for 'moody'. Unsurprising, therefore, that *kayf* has given us the North African *kif*, for cannabis. *Mazeje mish mnih* means 'I am not in a good mood (today).'

But it is when *keef* and *mazej* come together that we get something a little special. *Keef mazejak* literally means 'How's your mood?' but it is free of the pejorative connotation of 'moody', as it is usually asked in a spirit of empathy towards one's interlocutor – a small, non-judgemental nod to someone else's shifting state of mind.

In a famous song called 'Il Hilwa Di' (This Pretty One) by the early twentieth-century Egyptian singer-songwriter Sayed Darwish, *mazej* comes across as that part of the human psyche that is immune to wealth disparities, because it is nourished by beauty, the wonder of daybreak and the mercy of God, all of which are readily available to poor and rich alike.

# Mukhayyar aw Mussayyar

The plane is on the tarmac and passengers are still coming in. I could, in theory, get out of my seat, retrieve my suitcase from the overhead compartment, squeeze past the incoming flow of bodies and jostle my way down the aisle all the way to the bridge. I would ignore the disapproving look of flight attendants as I hurry back into the airport building, sprint all the way to the exit lobby, find a taxi and disappear into Beirut's much-loved alleys.

But I don't, because the later I leave it before making my volte-face, the harder it is to pull off. Every postponed second adds a new obstacle, another microscopic nudge that keeps me glued to my seat, continuing along the path I chose earlier. Hollywood may have popularised the image of a protagonist – an about-to-depart traveller or a soon-to-be bride – changing their mind at the very last minute in a spectacularly liberating moment, but how often has this actually played out in reality?

It is 6 August 1995 and the past few years have been rather dramatic – a woman I loved ended our relationship and overnight I lost all hearing in one ear. I resigned from my job in the New Forest, lost another one in Paris and was fired from a third in Beirut. Worst of all, that same year, Faber & Faber knocked back the manuscript of my first novel.

So here I am, leaving again, waiting for the plane to close its doors and take off. If there is much less conviction in my journey this time, compared to my first departure to London Heathrow nine years earlier, it is because I have been running out of options and emotional fuel.

I am heading east, not west on this occasion, flying over the Jordanian desert, onto the Indian subcontinent and the Indonesian archipelago, across the Timor Sea, above the vast and mostly empty Australian continent, all the way to Sydney, New South Wales.

My journey in the last decade is starting to look like a muddled script from the two World Wars. First, I flew over the Mediterranean, skirting the Gallipoli Peninsula, across the Germanic hinterland of Europe, up north towards the Western Front, the muddy trenches now covered with green pastures, before single-handedly invading the British Isles. Then, six years later, came D-Day, across the English Channel, and on to Paris, no resistance encountered apart from a sullen officer in Le Havre who gave me a resentful look before stamping my passport – clearly, I was not the kind of liberator he was hoping for. And now, my most ambitious move of all, landing on the Australian continent and taking on the Anzacs on their own turf, a feat no military power has ever attempted before ...

When, on an otherwise sunny day in 1992, a woman I loved, and had dated for a few months, broke up with me, I became an emotional wreck for a few weeks, and I needed a radical change of some kind. Within a couple of months, I had resigned from my job, stuffed my white Ford Escort with what was left of my belongings after I sold or gave away most of them, and driven to Paris, where my sister Hiam had been living for the past few years. I enrolled in a master's degree in environmental science – never mind that I was already in possession of a PhD; a master's degree seemed the easiest way to make the transition to a more fulfilling career. I landed myself a job at a research centre in Versailles, the Institut national de la recherche agronomique, funded with a post-doctorate research fellowship that doubled up, most conveniently, as my master's research project.

My move had the desired effect and within a few months I was on the mend – there was something cathartic about the tree-lined, softly lit streets of Paris, with their cafes, cinemas and patisseries; the easy cosmopolitan vibe of the city compared to the parochialism of the South of England; my reconnection with my Francophone self; a convivial work environment; Estelle, the fellow student that I was now dating; and, not least, Hiam's care and companionship.

Every morning, I would travel from Paris to Versailles, under a brilliant blue sky, in my right-hand-drive British car, remembering to keep on the right-hand side of the road, mostly. When I stopped at traffic lights, pedestrians would sometimes stare with puzzlement at the absence of the driver in my vehicle. And, just in case I did not take this hint about control and agency, fate soon sent me a much clearer message.

One day, I walked out of a cinema in Paris after watching a Dolby Stereo version of *Malcolm X* and noticed that I had lost all hearing in my right ear. I'd had the flu and a sore throat in the past two weeks but, by that stage, the pain was gone and I was feeling perfectly fine. I had suffered a moderate hearing loss in both ears over the past decade, for reasons unknown. But I had never experienced anything as remotely brutal as a complete shutdown of one ear.

After several weeks of intense medical attention that was almost as traumatic as the triggering event – emergency admission; multiple MRIs; half a dozen or so audiograms; steroid therapy, which flooded my bloodstream with cortisone; oxygen therapy, in which I was made to spend hours on end each day, for several consecutive days, in an *Apollo 11*-like capsule at a specialised medical facility, breathing through an oxygen mask; hospitalisation, in which an all-out antibiotic assault mounted on my body gave me non-stop hiccups for forty-eight hours – the doctors threw up their hands and admitted that they did not know what had caused the loss. It was most likely of genetic origins, they speculated, inherited from my father, who had a hearing loss that went back to his mother's side of the family. Exposure to the loud noise of explosives during the civil war would not have helped.

The damage was to the inner ear, not the hearing nerve: that much the doctors could tell me, although this knowledge did not seem to have any practical implication, not at the time. The only piece of information that *was* practical, albeit in a rather tragic way, was that there was every chance that my sudden hearing loss was irreversible, that no suitable hearing aids existed for me because my hearing loss was not uniform across frequencies, and that the prospect of losing hearing just as suddenly in the other ear could not be ruled out. In other words, I was always going to go partially deaf, my actions could only accelerate the process or slow it down, but not reverse or prevent it, and from now on I was a sitting duck for whimsical physiological destiny.

A disorienting asymmetry was now written into my aural anatomy, and not just my driving arrangements, which made socialising in groups strenuous, but I had better get used to it. Not long after, my contract at the institute came to an end. My work had gone well and the research, on the carbon cycle in forest soils, produced valuable insights and a paper that would become my most cited. But the research grant providing my salary had expired and there were no other funds available.

I packed my suitcase and returned to Beirut to take up a consulting position with the Lebanese Ministry of Environment. War in Lebanon had ended in 1990, reconstruction had started in earnest, there was much hope in the future and many emigrants like me were returning.

It took less than six months for the director-general to fire me. The corruption and graft at the ministry were jaw-droppingly blatant, at all levels, from routine quarry inspections in which developers bribed the ministry's engineers, all the way to high-level ministerial transactions.

Since I took no bribes and insisted on doing my job, I did not fit well in the environment. The writing had been on the wall for some time when the director-general walked into my office one day and dismissed me. Two years later, the man himself, along with a few other senior civil servants, would be convicted by a Lebanese court and jailed in an anti-corruption drive.

None of this would have mattered much had my writing gone as planned. I had started writing my first novel while still living in England and, by the time I moved to Paris, I had become completely immersed in it. The pleasure I drew from writing was unlike anything else I had experienced, and I became single-mindedly focussed on finishing the manuscript. When I did, I sent it to Robert McCrum at Faber & Faber with a recommendation from Beryl Bainbridge, who had read excerpts of it when I met her at a writing workshop in Wales.

I had enrolled in the workshop when I was still living in Paris, in order to seek feedback on my writing. Naively, I had thought that the good word of a well-known writer – winner of the Whitbread and Guardian Fiction prizes, and twice shortlisted for the Booker – was a certain path to publication. I wasn't even sure whether McCrum himself had looked at the manuscript or not, as I later found out that he had had a serious stroke around the same time. In any case, I only received the polite rejection letter from Faber after I moved to Beirut. I was now at a dead end, because trying to publish a novel in English while living in Beirut was close to impossible.

It was around this time that I received word from my sister Hiam that the Australian embassy in Paris had granted me permanent residence as a skilled migrant. I'd never been south of the equator before, but I had applied before leaving France on the advice of a friend who grew up in Australia and loved the place. I had lodged the papers out of precaution, more than anything, in case my return to Lebanon did not work out well.

So here I am on a plane, headed to Sydney. My mother has given me a long hug and kissed me on both cheeks, holding me for a few more seconds, tears streaming down her face. In her mind and for her generation, Australia, even more than America, is a continent one does not return from. She has bid farewell to more than half her children in the past seven years. She was overjoyed when I returned to live in Beirut and now, six months later, I am putting her through the pain again.

To my mystified friends in Beirut before I leave, I blurt out the usual clichés: 'getting a passport other than the Lebanese one', 'exploring possibilities', 'finding work', even 'a little adventure'. But the only reason I find remotely convincing in the silence of my mind is '"Why not?' My move is motivated by little more than a kind of long-time wariness that has settled over me in the past few months, a weakening of resistance to fate, a propensity to move with whatever life current happens to be shoving me this way or that, at the particular point in time when a decision can no longer be postponed.

To the age-old philosophical question of human agency, and whether individuals have the power to steer their own destiny or are driven instead by forces beyond their control – *mukhayyar aw mussayyar* in the charmingly concise Arabic articulation – I may have answered on that day that we are the willing, not-so-free agents of our own submission to fate, and that fate is little more than the inexorable 'rush of things' which our bodies know better than to resist, even as our minds scream in protest.

# The Lucky Country

Australia, at first sight, is another version of England. Not at second sight, though, and certainly not at third. One of the first indications to the newly arrived on the continent that this place is more than the projection of an English mind onto faraway shores, are the place names along the highway.

The Bay Run in Sydney's inner West at dusk.

Wollongong. Woolloomooloo. Wagga Wagga. Gadigal. Kogerah. Gangulu. Parramatta. Turramurra. Something about those names – the abundance of vowels, the oceanic ebbs and flows in the span of single words, the self-rhyming and the repetitions, the earthly 'gg' and the faintly mystic 'oo' – tells you that English is reaching the limits of its capacity to apprehend the place.

Welcome to Australia. A land rich in breathtaking landscapes and rare minerals and self-burning forests and Indigenous syllables. A place in which an ethos of equality and openness to the world coexist with vast disparities in wealth and deep-seated racism. This luckiest of countries – if one discounts those arriving by boat, and those who have been here all along, and those who are sleeping rough on the dark corners of Pitt Street, around Central Station and under the railway bridge in Wentworth Park, where I catch a glimpse of the darkness of a place otherwise full of sunlight and hope and invigorating goodwill.

# Old News

I am in Beirut on a visit. I meet up with an old friend at the Sporting Club. I haven't seen him in years. We dip into the quiet swimming pool, chatting and reminiscing.

'Have you heard about Mona?' he asks me out of the blue.

I haven't.

'She died while undergoing a Caesarean.'

I am stunned. I haven't seen Mona for many years.

I ask what happened.

'Complications from the surgery.'

We fall silent for a moment, then move on to a different subject.

# Mona

The Arabic root word *mona* (or *mounya*) has given birth to multiple, seemingly incongruous meanings. The most common occurrence is *umnia* or *mona*, for 'wish'. *Tamanna* means 'he wished'. My mother would sometime respond to a request by one of her children with *mona ayni* – 'my eye's wish' – as an emphatic yes. *Mona* can also take an active form in *manna*, to make someone want or wish for something.

But *mounya* has also given us *mouni'ya* and *mannaa* whose nearest English translation is 'befall'. *Mouni'ya bil fashal* is Arabic for 'he met with failure'. *Manaahu llahu bi'l hazeema* means 'God handed him a defeat'. *Maniyya* is also 'death', and, in plural, it becomes *manaya* and acquires another shade of meaning as 'difficulties' or 'vicissitudes', either encountered or self-inflicted.

It is not entirely clear to me whether all these variations come from the same root or whether some are homonyms. Regardless, every time I hear the word *mona*, each of those meanings flicker in my mind alongside the brighter image of the almost-friend of my childhood.

# Ring of the Dove

Ibn Hazm al-Andalusi – a polymath from eleventh-century Cordoba in Muslim Spain – wrote a treatise on love called *Ring of the Dove*. The titles of its thirty chapters are the nature of love, signs of love, loving in one's sleep, loving from a description, loving at first sight, loving but only after a long courtship, loving one quality (of the beloved)

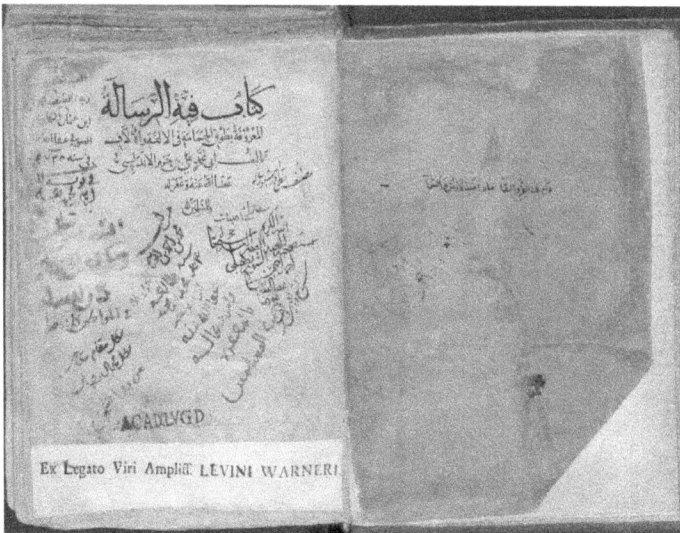

Opening page of manuscript of Ring of the Dove by Ibn Hazm al-Andalusi.

but not another, slandering, eye contact, correspondence, the messenger, keeping it a secret, broadcasting (it), obedience, disobedience, shaming, a helping friend, the watcher, denunciation, connection, abandonment, loyalty, double-crossing, separation, contentment, love sickness, peace of mind, death (from love or abandonment), the ugliness of vice, the virtue of abstinence.

# Future

I publish my first literary essay in *Heat*, a Sydney-based literary magazine. And then my second. A short story of mine appears in *Meanjin*, another literary magazine. And then an essay. Hodder Headline offers to publish my novel, and *Tell the Running Water* is launched at Gleebooks in 2001. A literary agent agrees to represent me in New York as does one in Sydney. My application for a new-writing grant from the Australia Council for the Arts is successful. The writing ship, it turns out, hasn't sailed after all. Australia is a land of hope.

# Precarity

First, one has to be careful with 'j' and 'g', their pronunciation in English almost the opposite of their French counterparts. Problem easily solved with a little application. Then there is the not-inconsiderable matter of the 'ch' and 'sh' syllables. The two letters 'ch' are pronounced 'tch' in English and 'sh' in French. With practice and persistence, years of French-language habits can be overcome.

Then there are all those silent letters in English, lurking, ready to ambush the unsuspecting speaker – the 'b' in *thumb* and *dumb*, the 'p' in *psychology* and *pseudonym*. For a language claimed by such a law-abiding people, English is replete with rule violation. It seems to take pleasure in exception. Either that or the rules are so complex as to be self-defeating.

In fact, for the non-native speaker, English is a slow process of finding out that you will never get pronunciation right, no matter how many years you spend interacting with the language. This is the native speaker's dirty secret, a far more effective marker of exclusive belonging than passports or blue blood. More pernicious, because it gives the aspirant the illusion of possible improvement, of getting there, almost, but never quite achieving it. A word, every now and then, is sure to put the naive outsider in his place. 'Oven' is not *auvein,* it's *aven.* 'Hitherto' is not *hai'thertoo.* Extrapolate from *Einstein* to *Weinstein* at your own risk.

The only fightback available is to act as if one doesn't care, or care enough. Or to go the other way when corrected by a native speaker, doubling down on mispronunciation and hurling it like an insult. I do this occasionally, but I know that such action is only available to those with enough cultural capital to stave off judgement. Besides, there is a limit to how much one can violate social norms, including those pertaining to languages, without paying a price.

I am left with a mild form of linguistic insecurity, entirely unreasonable but nevertheless real, a sense in which my mastery of the language is precarious and, like the Western passports of Middle Eastern dual citizens after September 11, revokable by faceless powers.

I have this idea that, when I learn a new English word, a new expression or a new turn of phrase, it becomes part of my writing arsenal and I can use it to say new things down the track, a month, a year or a decade later. Like a box of curiosities that I collect and can pull out and use any time I want. All the better if the box in this case is my own mind. It is there, safely under lock, and no one can take it away from me. All I need is to come across the word or expression for the first time, find out what it means from context or dictionary or both and, hey presto, it belongs to me.

All true, except for one crucial little fact. The box is leaky, words may vanish of their own accord, and there is no guarantee that next time I look for something I will find it. The science of retention defeats me, what stays and what vanishes from one's memory of a non-native tongue. So I resort to heuristics – that wonderful English word which I have to look up several times before my mind finally retains it – trying things out to see if they work, never mind why.

One thing does seem to work. When reading English fiction or non-fiction, I take to writing every new word or expression I come across in a notebook, so that I can come back and find it. Notebooks may not be quite as convenient as one's memory but at least they don't leak. Great technique – except that it interrupts the flow of my reading. Even more so when I realise that it's not enough to write down the word. I need to take in the full sentence in which the word has occurred, so that next time I consult the notebook I can work out the meaning without having to go back to the dictionary.

And it works, sort of. In time, my vocabulary grows, and more and more words start coming naturally to me, without having to go back to the notebook at the point of writing. But many words do not. Hardest of all is the panoply of suffixes running riot around words – *carve up, carve out, stand up, stand down, stand out, fold in, live up* – undermining my ability to extrapolate meaning, keeping me on my toes, sometimes even thumbing their nose at me, in this most effective form of linguistic power.

What lingers, in other words, no matter how slightly, is this sense that a second language is always a work in progress, always in need of improvement, and that one is always at a disadvantage compared to the native speaker, only able to wield the language as a prosthetic, never as a limb one is born with.

# The Names

The children's names were always going to be something of a sticking point. Perhaps because, in a cross-cultural relationship, of all potential objects of difference and disagreement, from the most trivial to the most serious, names were the most visible, with a once-and-forever finality to them.

As Ann became pregnant with our first child, and then our second, we had to agree on the matter of their names. We both wanted the children to carry our surnames, and it was desirable that their first or middle names paid tribute to one of our parents or grandparents.

My perspective came from a place of cultural pride and antagonism, a need to affirm my identity against Australia's prevailing sense of European superiority. Ann didn't want the children's names to become a burden to them and they had to be easy to pronounce by English speakers. We argued, half in jest: to the charge that my position was patriarchal, I responded that her feminism was distinctly Eurocentric. We teased each other too: Abu-Jaafar and Abdel-Salam were thrown around, inviting Ephraim and Reginald in response. Given the ancient religious connotations of many names in Arabic and English, there was no obvious meet-me-halfway position. The irony, not lost on anyone within a hundred miles of our social circles, was that Ann and I were uncompromising atheists.

Fortunately, we shared each other's concerns as well, which was a good basis for reaching a compromise. And then history happened and raised the stakes for Middle Eastern names.

# The September Years

Ali and Sami were born into a world full of promise. As the September 11 attacks and their aftermath changed the world, they strode happily into a decade of turmoil.

The Falling Man, New York, Twin Towers, September 11, 2001.

# Barbarians on the Loose

Within days of the September 11 atrocities, the United States invades Afghanistan, removes the Taliban from power in Kabul and dismantles much of Bin Laden's al-Qaeda infrastructure.

Less than two years later, the United States invades Iraq, after accusing Saddam Hussein of lying when he claimed to have destroyed his weapons of mass destruction. Widespread demonstrations in capitals around the world oppose the war. Cynical minds suspect the American government to be motivated by the economic and geopolitical benefits of access to Iraqi oil fields.

Within a few weeks of the launch of the war, the United States occupies Baghdad and President George W. Bush declares victory, to the delight of millions of patriotic Americans. But the celebrations turn out to be premature. A long, bloody war follows, in which crimes are committed by all sides. Pictures of American troops torturing Iraqi prisoners at Abu Ghraib shock but make little difference to the conflict.

By December 2011, American troops have withdrawn from Iraq. Deaths from the conflict at that point have reached anywhere between 150,000 and 600,000, depending on who's counting and how they count, with millions more injured or displaced. In the year leading to the United States' withdrawal, the new Iraqi government awards oil contracts to American, European and Chinese firms, and signs multi-billion-dollar agreements to purchase American weapons.

It turns out that Saddam Hussein, a man not usually known for his virtues, had been telling the truth all along about his weapons of mass destruction. A few years down the track, ISIS, a fundamentalist death cult, occupies vast stretches of Iraq, causing further death and mayhem.

In Palestine, the second intifada erupts in 2005, more violent than the first. It lasts five years with over 3,000 Palestinians shot by Israeli security forces and 1,000 Israelis killed by militant attacks and indiscriminate suicide bombings. Israel withdraws unilaterally from Gaza in 2005, after dismantling Jewish settlements in the strip, but maintains a land, air and sea embargo.

In Afghanistan, the Taliban engages American troops in a long-running war of attrition. In 2021, President Joe Biden decides to put an end to America's military involvement in Afghanistan and troops execute a hasty withdrawal, leaving behind many civilians who have worked with the United States-allied administration. The Taliban overrun the capital and seize power. One of its first acts of government is to ban girls from schools. The total number of fatalities in the war is estimated at more than 150,000.

It is said that the United States went to Afghanistan to remove the Taliban and now, twenty years and four American presidents later, has finally handed over power to ... the Taliban.

# Jihaad in Europe

In 2012, a middle-aged Lebanese couple, husband and wife, both well-respected professionals, were strolling towards X-ray security checks at a European airport, prior to boarding a flight. The husband was walking a little faster than the wife and was soon ahead of her. He was about five to ten metres from the X-ray machines, his wife another five metres or so behind him, when she wanted to say something to him.

'Jihaad ...' she called: his first name. He stopped, looked over his shoulder and was about to respond but had no time to do so. Security guards pounced on both of them, yelling and pointing guns. The guards – not unreasonably – mistook the wife hailing her husband for a war cry preceding a terrorist attack. Ironically, you could not think of a more peaceful-looking pair. Nor did their appearance give clues to their ethnic identity, except for a vaguely Mediterranean provenance.

The misunderstanding was ultimately cleared up, and the couple continued their trip unhindered. With the distance of time, they even saw the funny side of the story and told it with the retrospective light-heartedness it deserved. Nevertheless, Jihaad and his wife became more careful about pronouncing the name in public places in the West.

# Juhd

Contrary to general perception, the name Jihaad – pronounced *jehaad* (3I'ha:d), with an emphasis on the last syllable, rather than the '*jee*'had' sometimes heard on English-language media, jarringly to an Arabic ear – is not particularly religious or Islamic, not even an exclusively male name. None of the Jihaads I know, including my eldest brother, are religious. Some are Christian, and one is a Greek-Orthodox female friend.

*Jihaad* means striving, or struggling for something good, whatever it might be. For the devout, this could be the exemplary life. It comes from the root word *juhd*, for 'effort', which has sprouted several other words in Arabic, both secular and religious but rarely political. *Mujahid* is fighter but can also be someone who strives. A *mujtahid* is a high-ranking *aalim* or religious scholar who can practice *ijtihad*, interpretation of the scriptures, a privilege reserved for a small, highly educated elite. But more commonly, *mujtahid* is an adjective that means hard-working – my Arabic teachers sometimes scribbled *mujtahid* on my school reports. In the Quran, the word occurs in different contexts and, although it is often used to refer to militancy and war, it also lends itself to non-violent interpretations such as 'striving to lead a pious life'.

# Gifts of Return

In September 2000, Ann and I fly to Beirut with our infant boy. I have been offered a lecturing position at the AUB and decide to take a one-year leave from my job at the University of Sydney. Ann is on maternity leave from hers. And then we extend for another year, and then another. We live in an apartment on the leafy sandstone campus, overlooking the Mediterranean. Strangely, as the Middle East goes from one turmoil to another, Beirut is at its serene best, despite its

Campus of the American University of Beirut (photo by Ahmad El Itani, copyrights American University of Beirut).

traffic jams and power cuts. There is something profoundly fulfilling about this return to the playground of my youth, its spirited energy and inimitable sociality. And, most of all, the new friendships it gifts me, as if I am the fortunate beneficiary of an ancient ritual of hospitality.

My mother is delighted, now that I have not only returned, but have come bearing my own gifts of one beautiful young boy and then another. Until that is, it's time to return to Sydney for good and to take back parts of what I have given.

As I board the plane, I wonder what kind of relationship my children will have to my homeland, and whether bonds of kith and kin, of culture and mother tongues, can survive distance, and dominant languages and the turmoil of global politics.

# Tongue Tied

I am sitting on an almost empty bus heading to central Sydney when my son calls me. He is doing an Arabic subject at university, and he has an assignment to submit the next day. He has texted me a page of writing that we are discussing over the phone. He's uncertain about a few words and some grammatical constructions. Is 'sunset' *shurooq* or *ghuroob*? How do you say 'train tickets were expensive'? And what about 'I love going to the city'? Is it *bil-madina* or *ila'l'madina*?

It is mid-afternoon and, shortly after I pick up the phone, around thirty schoolkids, mostly teenagers in uniform, board the bus and quickly fill it up. I am still deaf in one ear, and my speech tends to be louder than average but not overly so – I know this from experience, even though I do not usually hear myself being loud. I notice some glances in my direction, every now and then. Those kids who seem to have noticed the conversation appear curious but not hostile, probably trying to work out what is this language I am constantly switching to in between my English sentences. I realise that I am being more self-conscious than I need to be. I chide myself for my innate caution, that I should be so mindful before speaking my own mother tongue.

There is of course a context to my self-consciousness about Arabic. Some of the more publicised instances of aggression against individuals from visibly or audibly Middle Eastern backgrounds have occurred on public transport. Head-scarves ripped off women's head, individuals verbally abused as they sat alone minding their own business, men forcibly removed from aeroplanes before takeoff because other passengers had been spooked by the Arabic they were speaking, reading or texting. In the minds of many, September 11 transformed Arabic into an enemy language.

Buses, trains and planes bring people into close proximity, and can make for intense encounters because passengers are in each other's personal spaces, either looking at each other or, more often, actively avoiding doing so. Our social interactions with strangers carry a latent threat of violence – even if most of the time we are not conscious of it – that we manage pre-emptively, through conventions about gaze, body language, and rituals of politeness and greetings. Growing up in the lawlessness of civil-war Beirut has left me with an added awareness of the ease with which the apparent civility of daily street life can give way to outbursts of tension, discord, even bloodshed.

I am a university professor, fluent in English, and while I still sometimes encounter racism inside and outside my work-place, it is rare, often subtle, and I am usually able to deal with it. I am fair-skinned and, like many dual nationals who migrated to the Western metropolis a long time ago, I do not stand out in public as particularly Arabic or Middle Eastern.

But my alien self can sometimes be *heard*. It is only when I speak Arabic or utter some Arabic expression, or when my name or that of my children is pronounced, that my other identity comes to the fore and becomes known to strangers. Each time I speak Arabic in public is therefore a watershed moment – low-key but dramatic – in which I have a sense that I am exposing myself to potential hostility. I work hard against this visceral affect and almost always overcome it, refusing to be cowed, insisting to myself on speaking Arabic in public, if and when it is expedient.

But something gives. Speaking Arabic becomes a small act of defiance in my own mind (and I suspect almost always *only* in my own mind) that robs me a little of the spontaneity of a mother tongue. So much so, I sometimes feel I am engaged in a double restitution – from the prejudice inflicted on the language by the world, and from my own self-consciousness when speaking it.

# FOUR:
# ANNALS OF LOSS AND HOPE

# Spring without Bloom

The Arab Spring erupts at the end of 2010 and spreads through most Arab nations. After giving rise to much hope, the protests unleash reactionary forces that double down on repression.

Regimes in Algeria, Morocco and Jordan, though shaken, remain in place. Those in Syria, Libya and Yemen resort to violent suppression of demonstrations, and plunge their nations into civil war. Within a few years, much of Syria lies in ruin as Bashar al-Assad, supported by Iran and Russia, wages a systematic war against the opposition, with indiscriminate bombing of civilian populations in rebellious cities, arbitrary detention, torture and murder. In Sudan, as a modus vivendi between protesters and the military junta breaks down, war erupts in Khartoum between two military strongmen and spreads to the rest of the country.

In Egypt, the jubilant scenes on Tahrir Square and the overthrow of General Husni Mubarak soon give way to darker times. The army, under General Abdel Fatah al-Sisi, removes the democratically elected Muslim Brotherhood president and shoots at protesters, and the state reintroduces mass incarceration and curbs on freedoms.

In Tunisia, where the Arab Spring started, a peaceful transition towards democracy appears to be in motion.

However, Kais Saied soon arrives on the scene, suspends the constitution and gives himself exceptional powers. The autocrat in this case is not an army general but, ironically, a constitutional lawyer.

In the Arabian Gulf, the violent clampdown has the tacit approval of Western allies, with the two core elements of the alliance – outflow of oil and inflow of military arsenals – continuing unabated.

It isn't long before ISIS spreads like a malignancy in the lawless stretches of Syria and Iraq, and stages attacks in Europe and the Middle East. In areas under its rule, summary executions, the enslavement of women and brutality are rife. Its violence is so nihilistic that the means cannot overwhelm its ends, because the means *are* the end, or at least a big part of it – to be seen perpetrating violence against one's perceived enemies and violators of its harsh codes of conduct.

In the meantime, Israel, American's closest ally, continues to run an apartheid regime in the occupied Palestinian territories. Wars erupt between Hamas and Israel every few years. In 2018, Gazan activists, backed by Hamas, organise the Great March of Return to the border with Israel, which consist of weekly, mostly peaceful, demonstrations close to the border fence. Israel responds with live ammunition and sniper fire, killing hundreds of demonstrators and injuring more than 13,000, the vast majority of whom are civilians with no connection to militant groups. The demonstrations continue until the end of 2019, causing much loss of life, with little to show for it.

The Lebanese civil war of 1975–1990 now looks like a mere rehearsal. Hundreds of thousands of Syrians, Iraqis, Yemenis and Palestinians have died and millions have been injured or displaced. Outmigration from countries of the

Levant is unprecedented. The Arab world is going from bad to worse. The scale of the loss, geographical and otherwise, is impossible to grasp. How does one find hope amid such devastation?

# Grief Palace

The shrouded body has been laid in the open-top box-shaped stretcher and left on display in one of the bedrooms for mourners to view. When the time comes, eight of us lift it and carry it through the gate and into the street, triggering shrieks by the women mourners. We set out in a procession of two dozen men, including the village imam, relatives, close friends, my brother Hekmat, old folks with long memories and young village lads with nothing better to do. We move slowly along the track leading to the cemetery. It's a ten-minute walk in the noon sun but it's mid-October and the worst of the summer heat is behind us.

Some pallbearers must be shouldering more burden than others because, though my palm is touching the underside of the coffin, there is no weight on my arms. I feel like an impostor, an alien in this world of unfamiliar rituals, but I remind myself that this is my father's funeral and that, in any case, everyone is foreign to death and mourning.

Every now and then, one of the bearers yells at the top of his voice: *Sallu ala Mohammad* (Pray for [the Prophet] Mohammad).

And everyone joins in: *Waa aalee Mohammad* (And the Prophet's kin).

The words sound strangely soothing, even to my atheist mind. When we reach the cemetery, my father's final resting place has already been dug and there, right next to it, is the gravestone – smooth white marble etched with starkly black ink – ready to be erected. We set down the stretcher, and two young men shift my father's body and carry it down into the hole, then climb out. Upon which, the imam, in his white cap and white robe, leaps athletically into the grave, bends over my father's head and whispers something in his ear. I am told, when I enquire later, that the imam's action was a *tal'eem*: instructing my father about what to say and what to do when he finally meets his creator. The dead, it turns out, can still hear the imam's words.

The imam climbs back up and we gather behind him as he stands facing the grave, lifts both hands to touch his temples and says the prayer of death. When the recitation is done, male members of the family, including my two brothers and I, stand in line to receive condolences from those present. Women will visit the cemetery later to say their prayers.

Meanwhile, the two young men shovel back the pile of reddish-brown soil over my father's shroud, which disappears under a shower of red earth. The formal word for soil in Arabic is *tharaa*. *Wourya tharaa* is to be delivered to the earth, that is, to be buried. From the same root is *tharaa'*, 'enrichment', and *tharwa*, 'wealth'.

It's 2016 and my father has died, aged 90. I flew to Beirut from Sydney the next day and arrived just in time for the funeral. I might have missed it altogether had I been a day later because Muslims believe burials should not be delayed beyond what is strictly necessary. I was picked up from the airport by my nephew and taken to my parents' apartment. I walked into a living room full of visitors offering condolences, and hugged my mother long and hard. Women in black and men in solemn suits, or more casual clothes, spoke to each other in hushed voices, never overshadowing the sad Quranic recitation playing in the background on a Bluetooth speaker.

I have attended three funerals in Sydney over the past few years, in churches and crematoria. The contrast with my father's funeral rituals could not be starker. In Sydney, rituals of death are predominantly about celebrating the life of the deceased and helping the bereaved accept the loss, right from the start. While normality might take a back seat for a few hours or a few days, it is always at the door, a smiling if dull presence, ready to walk into the room and usher the mourners back to the fold of the un-bereaved. It is as if the world's tolerance for solemnity is limited and must not be stretched.

In Beirut, almost everything in the rituals accentuates the otherworldly extraordinariness of death. Sometimes separate memorials are held for the deceased, especially for men of renown. But at funerals per se, no speeches are usually given extolling the qualities or quirks of the deceased and no endearing jokes are offered. It would appear that only the grim word of God – whether playing in the background or spoken by the imam – and the carefully executed rituals of movements and performances, can live up to the enormity of the event. The mourning period is protracted – there are specific rituals for the *thaleth*, the third day; the *usbu*, seventh day; and the *arbaeen*, fortieth day. Anything less would be seen as an undignified return to normality. Normality is there, of course, hard at work, making possible the very rituals that negate it, but never allowed to intrude too much, always out of view unless absolutely necessary, like a butler serving guests at a VIP dinner.

My thoroughly secularised mind finds affinity with the rationality of Sydney's take on death, and its classy aesthetics – the carefully orchestrated proceedings, the truncated biography, light-heartedly delivered, the crafted bon mot, the avoidance of overly demonstrative emotions and, not least, the occasional laughter tinged with sadness. But no matter who the deceased is, no matter how close to my heart, no matter how wonderful, brilliant, successful, generous, or all of the above, no matter how much she has achieved in her short or long life, when speeches end and proceedings close, as I get up and walk away, a tiny question – almost imperceptible beneath the larger emotions – nags at me. Is that it? Is that all there was to her? Perhaps because no summary could ever avoid becoming a summing-up, and the disappointing smallness of every human life is not quite what I, and other mourners, need at this point in time, still so close to the loss.

For all its irrationality, Beirut's approach to death, with its far sharper delineation of *dunia* (life) and *aakhira* (afterlife), speaks better to my grief. This may be because its rituals echo and amplify the devastation of bereavement, rather than try to dampen it, as I discovered at my father's funeral. The beloved, we are asked to believe, is now going to a different realm of existence, where the petty calculus of human affairs no longer applies, something of an entirely different order prevails; and there is much consolation, even hope, in that.

That the rational minds of non-believers like me do not accept this account is beside the point. After all, it is to our bodies that grief poses the hardest questions, and Beirut's rituals seem to always tell us quite precisely what to do with them. And once our bodies have entrusted themselves to the mysterious wisdom of the rituals – sights and sounds, words and gestures – the burden of our minds is made easier to carry.

# Mind and Body

The word for 'mind' in Arabic is *thihn*. The word for 'fat' is *dihn*. The letters 'th', ذ, and 'd', د, are almost identical in transcription: 'th' is basically 'd' with a dot added. Just a tiny dot. Not even a line or a dash separating mind and body. Hardly a dualism.

# Mohammad and Elias Walk into a Bar ...

My father told a joke once, about two well-to-do Lebanese men, Mohammad and his Christian friend Elias, who in the 1930s drove south from Beirut for a tour of Palestine. This was before the creation of the state of Israel and movement was more or less free along the eastern Mediterranean coastline. The two friends headed first to the Galilee and stopped at the ruins of Khirbet Cana. Elias told his friend about the village that once existed on this site, and about the day when Jesus turned up at a wedding – 'right here, in this very place, my friend' – and made water into wine.

The two tourists continued further south and, as they approached Bethlehem, Elias eased his foot off the acceler-ator and related to his friend, eyes sparkling with joy, the immaculate conception of Jesus, whose mother, the Virgin Mary, carried God himself in her womb for nine months. He told of the Three Wise Men who saw a sign in the stars, which guided them to a humble abode where they found the infant Jesus, recognised him for who he was and fell to their knees, worshipping him.

When the two friends reached Jerusalem, they parked the car in a backstreet and walked to the Church of Holy Sepulchre. Elias put his arm around Mohammad's shoulder and, his voice now charged with emotion, told him how Jesus was captured by Roman legions and pinned to a cross, with nails driven through the palms of his hands and a crown of thorns stabbed into his head; how he was made to shuffle down via Dolorosa, step by painful step, jeered at in these very same alleys; and, with a tear of joy now visible on Elias's cheek, how the son of God, despite the depredations inflicted on his body, rose miraculously from the dead three days later.

Mohammad knew the story of Jesus, of course, but he was touched by his friend's heartfelt account and had become almost equally emotional. He was a little confused as to whether Jesus was God or his son, but he was an open-minded man. There may be some rational explanation for this, he told himself and, in any case, it would not do to interrupt the story for such a trivial detail.

He hooked his arm to his friend's as they kept walking east, entranced by the sights, stepping lightly over the sun-drenched cobblestones. As the golden dome of al-Aqsa Mosque rose from behind a sandstone house, Mohammad told Elias how one night his own namesake, the Prophet, flew on a winged mare called Buraq from the Great Mosque of Macca to this very same site, whence he ascended to Heaven, met with God and greeted the ...

But Mohammad sensed a change of mood, and the hint of a scowl appeared on Elias's face. He stopped in his tracks and asked him what was wrong.

'Look, Mohammad,' Elias said a little hesitantly. 'You are a dear friend and a wonderful companion, but do you really expect us to believe this hocus-pocus?'

# Insight

My memories of my father are made of his lean figure and sunken eyes, his loving kindness, the immaculate suits he wore, the little I know of his traumatic childhood, as well as those Quranic verses promising salvation for those who believe.

After I left Lebanon, he would write to me every now and then, updating me on family news and the state of war in our beloved country. He would sometimes add a few lines cautioning me not to be seduced by Western technology, and not to lose my identity as an Arab and a Muslim.

Dad, I would respond in the silence of my mind, I am studying engineering: Western technology doesn't seduce me – it bores me. As for Muslim, I stopped believing in God a long time ago, as I am sure you know. And no need to worry, there is a part of being Arab and Muslim that never leaves you anyway, and for that I am thankful.

I see him sometimes, back in the days when we were both much younger, sitting next to me on the green velvet sofa in the living room of the apartment in which I grew up, on a cool winter night, French windows and wooden shutters closed to keep the warmth in, the crimson patterns on the carpeted floor shimmering bright under the two dozen tungsten lightbulbs of our bronze chandelier. Head bent,

Quran open in his lap, his forefinger traces a verse while reading it aloud for my benefit, something heart-warmingly gentle in his tone and manners. I watch the page and listen to the words being transformed by this sleight of voice – Judgement Day a little less judgemental, Hell less fearsome, the rivers of Heaven and the scales of Justice more enchanting.

I can still hear him probing the unsettled emotional landscape of my ten-year-old self, under the guise of God, philosophy and matters of life after death. What I see, in those moments now seared in my memory, is a space – made of words, chandeliers and the rustling sound of paper – in which a man and a child can speak about matters they otherwise did not know how to speak about. About angst and fear and the violence of the world, about loss, desire and hope, without ever saying the words, because men and boys – for whatever reasons to do with masculinity and

My father with his uncle Jaafar (right) and his cousin Abu Mustafa (left).

culture and other such peculiarities of the world – find it hard to do so.

And I now understand that, while faith – *imaan* – is belief in an idea, often a counter-intuitive one, it is almost always carried through a connection to a significant other. That faith almost always starts as belief in another human being – a peculiar form of love – which is then transformed, through abstraction and language, into something bigger.

Arabic, in my case, has been the principal vehicle of this transformation and, while the ideas themselves (God and heaven and suchlike) have long lost their substance for me, their imprint in my mind remains – a privileged insight of some kind, something resembling a healing, but with no memory of a wound. Something that, whatever it is, is intrinsically bound to my mother tongue.

# Najwa

Najwa is a female name in Arabic, slightly old fashioned but still current in many Arabic-speaking countries. It comes from the root word *naaja*, 'to reveal (one's secret to someone)'. *Najwa* has several interrelated meanings. One is the hushed and intimate conversation between two individuals. Another is the internal monologue that sometimes one has with oneself. A related word is *munaajaat*, which is often used to refer to a poetry genre in which the author addresses him or herself to God. A homonym of *naaja* is *najaa*, which means 'to escape (from death)'. *Najaa* has also given us a female name, Najaat, which means 'salvation'.

# Speech

Arabic has the same word for 'speech' and 'modern', *hadeeth*, and there is a lingering sense that modernity has as much to do with what one says as with what one does. *Hadeeth* comes from the root word *hadath*, 'event', or *hadatha*, 'happened'. At its simplest, *hadaathah*, 'modernity', is that which has happened recently, rather than the more prevalent meaning it has come to acquire, namely a radically different, utterly superior, European-inspired way of doing things and viewing the world.

In Islamic philosophy, *muhdath* is a reference to all that is created, falls within history, and hence stands in opposition to the eternity of God. There is also 'the Hadeeth', with a capital 'H' in English, even if Arabic has no such thing as a capitalised version of letters. The Hadeeth is a collection of sayings attributed to the Prophet Mohammad and sanctified as canon. It is a major source of jurisprudence in Islam.

Dwelling in this most solemn company is a much less pretentious, easily overlooked word, found in the Egyptian dialect of Arabic – *haddoutha*, meaning a very short story, a fairy tale or simply an anecdote, while *hawaadeeth* is its equally delightful plural. To an Arabic ear, *haddoutha* sounds like a term of endearment or a word invented by the lively mind of a lisping five-year-old.

# Hawaadeeth

'Tell me again about your father sailing to Africa, then marrying off your sister to an old man,' I sometimes start, speaking to my mother, recalling something she has told me a long time ago but whose details have become hazy in my mind. That is all I have to say to launch her into an hour or so of remembrance and storytelling. She is in her eighties and often speaks to me about her childhood. When I visit Beirut to spend some time with her, usually once a year, she regales me with stories from the world in which she grew up.

Our conversation is made more intense by the limited time we usually have at our disposal, since I usually only stay for a week or two before returning to Sydney. We sit at one end of the long and narrow balcony of her apartment to have our morning coffee together – she likes the thick Arabic brew and I am partial to an espresso. Beirut is just waking up, the street still serenely quiet at this time of the day.

I listen to my mother and my fondness for her grows as I watch her speak. I wonder at her capacity to keep alive a sense of youth by dwelling on, and playing with, shards of broken dreams and enduringly strong emotions from long ago. Always a twinkle of teenage self and nostalgia in her eyes – she is still flattered by memories of the flirtatious attention she received in her twenties and thirties, when she was already a mother to five or six children. Wrinkles have taken hold around her eyes and pull at the corners of her thin-lipped mouth, but the skin on her cheekbones is largely intact, as if her face, battered by life and its struggles, has reached a compromise with time.

She has had her fair share of grief, dislocation and abandonment. Her body survived the rigours of seven pregnancies in eighteen years, with the first newborn lost to illness as an infant. She raised, with my father, six children, amid civil strife and violence, and lost her mother in the war. And yet, here she is, I tell myself, more or less at peace with herself, happy to dwell on the past, still alive with desire and cheeky humour.

The stories she tells me are fascinating, not just her own but those of the larger world of the 1930s and 1940s to which she once belonged as a child: there was something darkly Victorian about that time, with its prudishness, its obsession with appearances and honour, its fear of social shaming, and the patriarchal hypocrisies that seemed to pervade it. It was a world that, for all its rigid conservatism, could not suppress stories of incest, sexual predation, honour crimes and substance abuse, even street prostitution and, later, in the glittering sixties and seventies of Beirut, its high-class counterpart.

In one story from the 1930s that my mother relates to me on one of these mornings, a woman reluctantly agrees to a request by her husband that his two seven-year-old daughters from a previous marriage move in with them. The biological mother of the two girls is from a poorer background and of lower social status. True to fairy-tale form, the stepmother gives them the most menial house chores. On one occasion, she punishes them for some transgression by leaving them hanging by a rope, wrapped around their bellies, in an empty well. One day, the stepdaughters, now teenagers, run away from home together. Their aggrieved father scours south Lebanon, looking for them without success.

It turns out the two sisters have parted ways soon after escaping. The older one heads south to Palestine, marrying a good man, raising a family and ultimately settling in Jordan after the *nakba* and the exodus of 1948. One day, the father is in Haifa when he is approached by a man who turns out to be his son-in-law. Father and daughter are happily reunited.

The younger sister, on the other hand, has travelled north to Beirut to join her biological mother and, years later, rumours reach the village that she has fallen in with disreputable company and that, helped by her mother, she has even prostituted herself – although whether this is meant literally is not clear. Her half-brother seeks her out to cleanse the shame she has inflicted on the family name. But this is his first trip to the big city and, confused, he ends up shooting the wrong woman. He goes to jail, where he becomes a drug user and dies from his addiction.

As I listen to my mother, I wonder whether she might have enlivened the tale, knowingly or not, perhaps confusing part of it with storylines from some Egyptian drama she watched on TV a long time ago. It's possible, but I am always struck by how rich with plausible details are the stories, and how well they fit with what I know about the places and times she comes from. Besides, I decide, such doubts are beside the point. After all, whatever the truth behind it, no other story I have ever heard has offered me such a delightful mix of Charles Dickens, soap opera and the Coen brothers, all set in the rustic alleys and gentle hills of south Lebanon, almost a century ago. What more can one ask from one's mother in her old age?

# Neither Red, Nor Yellow

It's 5 August 2020 in Sydney and, when I wake up, there is a brief text message from my niece who lives in Melbourne. 'Everyone is safe', the message says, which worries me, as I have no reason to believe that anyone isn't.

Lebanon has a habit of springing surprises on its citizens every few years, usually in the form of calamities that exceed our imagination. I turn on my computer with some trepidation and wait for Windows to load so that I can check the news. It is supposed to be a normal day, even if normality itself has undergone a decisive shift over the previous few months, thanks to COVID-19. Something momentous is happening in the world – entire cities in lockdown, businesses collapsing, lives lost, livelihoods shattered.

Melbourne has just gone back into lockdown, even though its infection rates are on much lower scale than in Europe, the United States, India and Brazil. In Sydney, we watch cautiously, still hopeful that we can avoid the worst of the pandemic. We are still more or less free to go as we please, so long as we stay clear of the airport. It appears as if, just as in World Wars past, Australia is perched a safe distance from the epicentres of a historical event and has escaped the worst of a global calamity. This belief does not come naturally to me: I am inclined to believe that history is something you endure and, if you're lucky, survive – escaping it is not usually on the menu.

My frail eighty-six-year-old mother is social-distancing in her apartment in Beirut. My annual trip to Lebanon cannot happen this year as the Australian government has closed the nation's borders, and I am a little worried that something might happen to her before I can see her again. At least she is safe and well looked after; under Covid, it is no worse to be in Beirut, Bogota or Bombay, than in New York, Sydney or Paris. Or so I think.

On the evening of 4 August, around six o'clock Beirut time – shortly after midnight in Sydney – two explosions, about thirty seconds apart, destroyed the city's port. The first, smaller explosion led to the second, massive blast – the detonation of a stash of around 3,000 tonnes of ammonium nitrate, which unleashed on the city an explosive charge equivalent to about a tenth of the atomic bomb dropped by the United States over Hiroshima. It tore through a large stretch of the city and was heard as far away as Cyprus, two hundred kilometres across the Mediterranean. The blast happened two days short of the seventy-fifth anniversary of the Hiroshima bomb, and almost exactly one hundred years after Lebanon was officially born as a nation state, on 1 September 1920 – two ironies not lost on Beirutis.

Over the next few days, it would emerge that hundreds were killed, thousands were injured, scores were missing and tens of thousands were homeless. The ammonium nitrate, which can be used as fertiliser or mining explosive, had been stored at the port for six years, in a staggering act of criminal negligence and institutional ineptitude, even by the poor standards of Lebanese officialdom.

The cloud of smoke that erupted was caught on camera and beamed around the world. There was something monstrously amorphous about it, in stark contrast to the well-defined contours of the mushroom cloud we associate with nuclear weapons. Notwithstanding the vast difference in their respective scales, both were terrifying in their own ways but one suggested unpredictability and chaos, while the other spoke of deliberation and planning.

The Japanese physician Michihiko Hachiya, writing in his diary about the horrific aftermath of Hiroshima, reported a civilian volunteer talking to him about the "beautiful cloud ... neither red nor yellow ... clear-cut as if a straight line had been made in the clear blue sky". No one, as far as I know, spoke in such terms of the Beirut cloud.

I called my niece in Melbourne – it was morning in Sydney and still the middle of the night in Lebanon, so I couldn't speak to Beirut. She'd rung her parents in Beirut shortly after the explosion. It turned out that members of our immediate families who were in the city at the time were all fine (most of my siblings, and their children, had settled overseas over the years). Their homes had sustained different degrees of damage, with broken glass and ripped-off window and door frames.

It was impossible to know, so soon after the event, if my many friends in the city were safe. The American University of Beirut had sustained significant damage. Over the next few days, I would find out that no one I knew personally was hurt. The only fatality I knew of, albeit with one degree of separation, was a friend of another niece of mine who had died from flying glass in his home. The apartment of a cousin of mine was destroyed in the blast. She lived in part of the Ashrafieh suburb overlooking the port but, fortunately, she and her husband were not at home at the time of the explosions.

My mother had a close call. She was sitting on the balcony of her apartment, on the third floor of a seven-storey building, when she heard the first explosion. She got up, leaned on her walker and took short, painfully slow steps into the house. Thirty seconds or so later, as luck would have it, she was halfway into the living room when the second blast shook the house, and the balcony became a mess of broken glass. With her chronically weakened blood circulation, diabetes and cardiovascular disease, it's unlikely she would have survived had she still been outside.

# Anatomy of a Collapse

The Beirut port disaster could not have come at a crueller time for Lebanon. The country was already in the throes of the worst economic and public-health crises in its history, with the local currency in freefall against the US dollar, the banking sector in disarray and depositors prevented from accessing their savings. Over the previous decade, the Central Bank had run a fiscal policy that amounted to a Ponzi scheme, in which it offered astronomical interest rates to private banks. In effect, deposits were being siphoned off to fund soaring and patently unsustainable public debt, to the benefit of an alliance of private banks, corrupt officials and high-powered politicians.

Dysfunctional institutions, in a country of three million people, were barely coping with over one million Syrian refugees, not to mention the hundreds of thousands of long-term Palestinian refugees and their descendants. Europeans were providing aid – partly out of fear of yet another exodus of Syrian refugees across the Mediterranean – but it was hardly enough. Poverty and unemployment soared, and the daily rate of Covid infections was rising again, after an early period in which the government had managed to keep it in check. If this was not enough, the Americans and Saudis were battling the Iranians for influence in a country whose political system had always been pathologically open to foreign interference.

The anti-government, anti-corruption protest movement that had started nine months earlier, demanding and promising change, had lifted the spirits of most Lebanese, including those like myself watching from afar. A new generation of young Lebanese women and men had asserted itself, rejecting the political system of graft, patronage and nepotism that had ruined the country. And they had done so with such force and creative energy – outwitting security forces with ever-changing forms of protest, harassing corrupt politicians who dared show their faces in public to the point that most had disappeared from public view, combining protests with street cleaning, tree planting and democratic forums – it appeared that, just for once, real change might be in the offing.

But in the weeks leading up to the blast, the protests had stalled. This was partly due to pandemic restrictions on movement and a mounting reluctance among the population to take to the streets. Equally to blame was the movement's inability to produce political leadership that could provide a viable alternative to the status quo, a failure that seemed to mirror that of other comparable protest movements around the world, from the Arab Spring to Occupy Wall Street in New York. The Lebanese movement was calling for the replacement of the entire political class – *killun yaani killun*, 'everyone means everyone', was its most famous motto – but it was not clear how this could happen and who would replace our inept politicians.

The political system had shown itself to be remarkably adept at reproducing itself. Almost literally: no kudos to any 1980s or 1990s futurologist reading a list of leading politicians of the time and extrapolating their 2020s equivalents. Chamoun and son. Hariri and son. Murr and son. Franjieh and son. Gemayel and son. Jumblat and son. Moawad and son (through interim, care-taking widow, until son grew up). Aoun and son-in-law (no son in existence). The 2040s list is already well on its way – Berri's son, Jumblat's son, Franjieh's son, and on it goes.

In Beirut, you often heard people, from taxi drivers to press commentators, blaming the country's problems on the *Nizaam* – a word which, in other contexts, means 'regime' or 'police state', but in Lebanon means 'system' or 'order', and does not carry the same connotation of police brutality and repression. Unlike the first meaning, in which it is usually easy to separate victim and perpetrator, the second embroiled everyone in corruption. Sectarianism and clientelism turned ministries into fiefdoms for political factions and trapped citizens in a culture of dependence on their political leaders for the basic necessities of life. Worse, it mutated into a pernicious culture of law-breaking and petty corruption, in which almost everyone was both prey and predator – from double parking on the street because traffic policemen were erratic in handing out tickets to stealing electricity from the public utility and not paying tax. The public good had become depleted, and everyone was poorer and more miserable for it.

The Beirut port explosion was a sobering moment for the deeply divided nation and quickly led, after a resurgence of protests, to another government resigning. Fingers pointed in all directions – the Lebanese presidency, Israel, Hezbollah, successive governments of prime ministers Saad Hariri and Hassan Diab, the port authority. Many wished for one of these accusations to stick, if only to avoid facing the truth. After all, we knew how to hold grudges and to hit back against enemies who meant us harm, but it was much harder to deal with the corruption and incompetence in our midst. Some called for a UN inquiry, while others insisted on a national one. A high-profile committee was formed by the government, and arrests were made. Investigating teams from France, Britain and the FBI arrived on the scene and presented their reports to Lebanese judges.

To glimpse how diabolically dysfunctional the Lebanese state had become, one need only take a peek at the transcripts of interrogations of officials responsible for the unloading, storage and management of the ammonium nitrate, as reported in the Lebanese press. They read as a litany of failures foretold. Ambiguously overlapping responsibilities by several competing government departments, including the port authority, the customs authority, the ministry of public works, a number of security agencies and the Lebanese army; staggering nonchalance by individual officials; several warnings issued about the stash of explosives over the years and ignored by successive governments.

The Lebanese public administration, first created in the 1920s, had been modelled on its highly bureaucratic French counterpart then, over the following hundred years, made a hundred times worse by graft, corruption and slow efforts at modernisation.

Underlying all this, as every Lebanese knew, was a sectarian system in which public-sector jobs were rarely given on merit, and mostly distributed as shares among 'sects' – Sunnis, Maronites, Shias, Greek Orthodox, Druze. In truth, 'sectarianism' served an alliance of politicians, conservative clergy and bankers, who ran an all-too-Lebanese form of kleptocracy, founded on patriarchy and crude economic laissez-faire.

But where did this sectarianism come from and why does Lebanon seem to be the only country afflicted with it in the region, at least to this extent? Part of the answer lies in Lebanon's geography and the way it had helped shape its history. Lebanon was unique along the eastern Mediterranean in that, though it was located under fifty kilometres from the Syrian hinterland and the desert, its territory included snow-capped mountain chains, up to three thousand metres in altitude, remote valleys and once-dense forests, only a day's ride from thriving trading posts on the Mediterranean. The difficult terrain meant that, throughout their history, these lands had been sought as a refuge by minorities escaping persecution by a succession of empires – Byzantine, Abbasid, Mameluke, Ottoman and, in the twentieth century, French and British.

So much so, by the time the Greater Lebanon rabbit was pulled out of the French hat, courtesy of the League of Nations, a century ago, it turned out to be a mosaic of religious sects that had made their home in its plentiful mountains and valleys. And, given their proximity to the Mediterranean, for hundreds of years, but especially through the nineteenth and twentieth centuries when Mount Lebanon became a zone of French influence, people with different beliefs and sectarian affiliations would come together in Beirut, Tyre, Sidon and Tripoli, to trade with each other and with the rest of the world. This was, after all, what these cities knew how to do best, for millennia, possibly back to the times of the Phoenicians. The fierce sense of independence of historically persecuted minorities in its countryside, combined with a clan-based mercantile ethos in its cities, produced in modern Lebanon a rich, generous, open-to-the-world blend of Arabic, European and Mediterranean cultures – something we Lebanese were rightly proud of and liked to see as our true selves.

Unfortunately, this recipe also turned out to be a rather poor formula for twentieth-century nation building, especially in a region riven with conflicts, mass refugee movements and imperial ambitions. This point was made, loud and clear, when the two tonnes of ammonium nitrate exploded at the port on that fateful Tuesday afternoon. It was as if some cruel, violent and truth-speaking God – assigned to us by a cruel, celestial League of Nations – wished to put paid, once and for all, to one hundred years of illusions that we, the Lebanese, liked to entertain about ourselves.

# Mind Games

I speak to my mother on the phone once or twice a week. Everything is much more expensive now, she tells me, although she doesn't sound too concerned, partly because my youngest sister, Maha, manages her finances, and my mother never looks at the balance sheet. Far more pressing for her is the day-to-day bickering with Sisi, her carer, a young Ethiopian woman, smart, reliable and strong-willed, who is doing a great job of looking after my mother.

'She's too stubborn!' my mother complains. 'Never does what she's told.'

She asks me about Covid in Australia – she has heard about the lockdown in Victoria. I say that New South Wales is fine. I don't say that our rate of daily infections is now hitting twenty and causing anxiety. Neither do I say that there is a sense that we might be heading Victoria's way.

She tells me about my seventy-five-year-old uncle Abdel Ameer, her younger and only remaining sibling. They have always been close – it was she who introduced him to his wife, Effat, in the early seventies, summoned him from Tyre to Beirut to meet the beautiful woman from Bint Jbeil who was studying for a college degree in Beirut. The pair fell in love and married soon after.

My mother (right) with her brother Abdel Ameer and his wife Effat, shortly after their marriage (early 1970s).

Abdel Ameer is a big-hearted and wonderfully generous man, whose dementia has worsened of late. He called her yesterday saying that he was about to go and fetch their mother, and could she please let him know where their mother was. She reminded him that their mother died forty years ago and that he buried her with his own hands.

'We're all declining one way or another,' I say, trying to console my mother. In reality, I am relieved that she at least, though eight or nine years older than him, is still in full possession of her mental faculties and that, for all the inevitability of decline, biology is also a game of chance in which sometimes you do get lucky.

For as long as I can remember, my mother, like most Lebanese, has had to pay, in addition to state utility bills, private providers of bottled water and small-generator electricity to make up for the frequent cuts to services, and prices are now soaring. My mother's carer will return to her homeland next month. Her salary, which my mother pays in US dollars, has shot up overnight. It is now equivalent to twice my mother's government pension, paid in Lebanese pounds, up from a third.

Now that my mother understands how expensive the carer has become and that she can no longer really afford her, she resents her even more and the bickering intensifies. It doesn't help that the two of them are locked in the apartment twenty-four hours a day, observing strict pandemic isolation. To make matters worse, rumours are rife that medicines are fast disappearing from pharmacies because of stocks destroyed in the explosion and the IMF putting pressure on the government to withdraw subsidies. This would be lethal for my mother, who depends for her survival on a hefty cocktail of drugs.

Three of my siblings and I meet over Zoom to discuss how to deal with all of this. We do have a few options, but it is hard to enact them amid bank closures and pandemic conditions. As we consider our options and toss around alternatives, it is clear that the world as we know it has shifted decisively in the last few weeks. We are each coping fine in our own corner of the globe, but it is my frail mother who appears to be trapped, almost alone, at the epicentre of several overlapping calamities.

I am in the kitchen making dinner while talking to my mother on WhatsApp. Victoria has just lifted the most stringent of its restrictions. Infection rates in both Victoria and New South Wales have been down to single digits for a couple of weeks. This is largely due to the hard work of frontline workers and contact tracers, but it still feels as if we have ridden our luck.

My mother tells me about the new carer that my sister, arrived in Beirut from Paris two weeks ago, has hired for her.

'She's too slight – I don't know whether she can do the job,' she complains. My mother still associates physical stature with strength of character and intelligence, against all empirical evidence. Still, this is a new item on her long list of carer criticisms.

I tell her that we're doing well now, things are looking up and that our federal health minister is talking about the real prospect of Covid vaccines. We share a joke about how many decades it will take for them to arrive in Lebanon. As it happens, Lebanon would prove to be ahead of Australia and, a few weeks later, she would get her first shot of a Pfizer vaccine on the same day as our prime minister, Scott Morrison, would get his, at the start of the Australian vaccination campaign.

She asks me what am I cooking today and I say mujaddara – a traditional rice and lentil dish, with fried onions sprinkled on top, that she taught me how to make. I tell her that I never seem to be able to match the crispiness of her onions. She gives me some advice about it – frying them in hotter oil and letting them sit in a strainer for a while. I ask her about Uncle, and she says he's still waking up in the middle of the night, asking about his mother. Once again, I feel grateful that Mum's mind is untarnished. We talk about Covid again for a minute or so. Then she asks me what am I cooking today.

# Untouched

I am going over the aerial photos of the port destruction that came out over the hours and days following the explosion. There is something apocalyptic about the devastation it left behind. The port – a platform of concrete sticking out into the Mediterranean, in a city that is itself a promontory – is in ruins, still smouldering, a spectacle of mangled steel, collapsed cranes and crushed concrete.

Most conspicuous are the dozen or so grain silos, or what's left of them, half-destroyed, half-eroded, vertical structures that have, ironically, absorbed some of the explosive charge, shielding parts of the city to the west. The bows of two ships – as stricken as the landscape around them – lean slightly against each other, like two bodies seeking solace in each other before dying. A massive crater, where the depot with the ammonium nitrate once stood, has bitten into the land, leaving behind a pool of turbid water in the shape of the upper part of a horseshoe.

But what I find most remarkable about the aerial photos is how peaceful the Mediterranean appears, how untouched by the calamity. In some photos, the water is scintillating aquamarine, in others deep blue, but never anything less than beautiful and serene.

The Eastern Mediterranean.

Perhaps one day, well after the world's capacity for hubris and violence has run its course, the deep and shallow seas, the mountain peaks and the steep valleys will still be there, ready for another start. Long after my mother and I and everyone else in the stricken city has gone. Long after biology has run its course, and long after history and petty politics have become nothing more than a footnote in a long-forgotten book. A sad consolation, if ever there was one.

# And Then There Were None

The morgue of Hotel Dieu – God's Hostel – is located at the back of the hospital grounds, in a separate section, with its own curved driveway, sparsely furnished lobby and cream-coloured walls. 'Hotel Dieu' is an old-fashioned generic French name for a hospital, dating from medieval times, but this connection between disease and religion, death and divinity, still resonates in the modern world. And it happens to be the official name for this hospital in the Ashrafieh district of Beirut that was, during the worst days of the civil war, a major trauma centre, like its namesake in Paris.

Hiam and I drive from our house, ten minutes away, to say goodbye to my mother and meet up with the funeral director who will be collecting her at the same time and looking after her over the next twenty-four hours – washing her body according to Islamic ritual, saying prayers over her and, the next morning, transporting her in a hearse for burial in Jibsheet, about ninety minutes away. We refer to him as the hajj, the honorific applied to any man, especially an older one, who has been on a pilgrimage to Macca. It can be confusing – several hajj will be present at the funeral, in one capacity or another – but it's just as well: one fewer name to remember in a week where we will be interacting with a slew of solicitous strangers.

We find the hearse, a gleaming-black Buick, already parked in the driveway. The hajj, a slight man with thick glasses, three-day stubble and a suitably solemn face that must have aged faster than his years, is leaning against the passenger door, talking to his assistant, a young man in jeans and white sneakers. After the customary greetings, Hiam exchanges a few words with the hajj, agreeing that we will have a few minutes to see my mother while they wait outside, after which they can get on with their job.

We walk into the empty lobby. Hiam grabs the handle of the heavy door, pulls it open, and leads the way into the mortuary room. The clerk, in light-blue surgical gown and full protective gear, is standing next to a small bed, on which lies the bundle of a body covered with a white sheet from head to toe. I am terrified by my mother's change in stature – is my mind playing tricks or has she been shrunk by pain, disease or death? – and for a moment I want to turn around and walk away.

The clerk exchanges brief looks with us – are you ready for this, his eyes ask. He folds back the top of the white sheet with both hands, slowly, almost ceremoniously, and reveals my mother's face. Her eyes are closed but her eyelids seem delicate, a gossamer softness to them. Her lovely golden complexion is still recognisable, but has started to fade into pale white. Her cracked lips have parted a little, making an 'o' shape. I am breathless for a moment, stunned by the sight of her lifelessness. It's been nine hours since I learnt that she died but I have not yet fully grasped the fact.

Hiam and I walk out of the mortuary room into the lobby, followed by the clerk, silently, as if any further conversation must be done out of earshot of the deceased. Hiam hands out a few banknotes to the clerk, discreetly, her hand hanging vertically by her side, briefly touching his, and receives a nod of appreciation in return. She exchanges a few final words with the hajj – what will happen to Mum's body tonight, at what time will the convoy south start tomorrow – and confirms payment arrangements. There is something both profane and reassuring about the quiet financial transactions that accompany death – the clerk looking after the body in Hotel Dieu expecting a tip, the funeral director setting his price with a hushed voice, fees to be paid to the waiter serving mourners the next day in Jibsheet, the grave digger, the gravestone carver and so on.

Profane, because death is so extraordinary that part of me expects the world to stop functioning the way it does, at least momentarily – in protest, in deference or in awe, I am not sure – and when it does not, this part of me is a little affronted. Reassuring, because money changing hands reminds me that death is not so extraordinary after all and that, for all the devastation I may feel, men and women go through it and come out the other end. What better proof than the way others who have not known my mother take her death in their stride and continue with the normal course of their lives? After all, I remind myself, people we don't know die every day around us, without us taking any notice.

In the car, I am still haunted by my mother's face, her small-ness, her delicate eyelids, her open mouth. A memory comes back to me of something she used to say about how, at the moment of death, a person's soul escapes from their body through their mouth. I have always been a little intrigued by this insistence on the materiality of the soul – why would it need an open passage to escape – even by some of those who believe in non-material existence. Isn't the soul precisely that which is of other-than-material essence, whatever it is, and would it not be *free* of physical laws? Isn't that the whole point?

I break the silence and tell Hiam that I am still reeling from seeing our mother lifeless. She says that what she saw on my mother's face was not lifelessness but peace and relief, and I find the thought comforting. Hiam had been living with, and looking after, my mother in the last four months, after she had another fall and her health started deteriorating fast. My three sisters, Hiam, Fatima and Maha, have seen my mother's suffering firsthand recently. Maha, the youngest, lives in Beirut and has been her long-term carer. My brother Hekmat visits Lebanon several times a year, while my eldest brother, Jihaad, also lives in Beirut. I, on the other hand, had not seen her since 2019.

It is only thirty-six hours ago that I woke up in Sydney and found a message on my phone from Hiam, asking me to call her. Mum had gone into septic shock overnight – a potentially fatal condition in which infection causes dangerously low blood pressure and can lead to multiple organ failures – and was in intensive care. This was Friday, 29 October 2021, three days before Covid-free vaccinated Australians would be free to travel again. To be allowed to leave before Monday, I needed a letter from the doctor stressing how critical was her condition. It was already close to midnight in Beirut, so I was lucky to catch our family doctor, who was also a good friend. He had just seen my mother at Hotel Dieu and was driving home. Mercifully, he was able to send me the letter within the hour.

I applied online to the Australian government and received authorisation two hours later. I purchased a ticket and quickly made arrangements for my absence from the university – my PhD students, my laboratory research and the subject I was teaching – mindful that internet access would not be straightforward in Beirut, what with the frequent power cuts. I was on the plane by 4 p.m. the same day. At Dubai airport, I met up with my niece and we caught the same flight to Beirut. We landed at 6.30 in the morning,

Beirut time, and, while we were waiting for the luggage, she called Hiam on her mobile phone. That was when I found out that I had missed my mother by less than two hours. She had died at dawn on the morning of my arrival.

The hajj's funeral room happens to be located in the Ghobairi neighbourhood, in the southern suburbs of Beirut where my mother and my father lived when they moved to the city from south Lebanon, over sixty-five years ago. This was where the hajj would be taking her body today, before driving it tomorrow to the apartment in the Ras al-Nabaa neighbourhood where my father and mother eventually settled: the one where I grew up, and where my mother lived for the last fifty-five years of her life, until her death. The hearse will arrive at 10 a.m. with my mother's body in the coffin, so that it can lead a convoy of about six or seven family cars, heading to Jibsheet.

So it is that, over the next twenty-four hours, my mother will be tracing in reverse a rough approximation of her life's journey, which started more than seventy years ago, when she was abruptly pulled out of her happy teenage existence in the village of Sh'hoor and sent off with a stranger who took her to his own village of Jibsheet, some thirty kilometres away, a depressingly vast distance for a suddenly disempowered girl, given that transport in those days was still mostly by mules and horses.

Tomorrow, she will first be taken to our ancestral house in Jibsheet, where she made many happy memories over the years, and where her body, resting in an open casket, will be placed in the main living room, on display for an hour or two, with Quran recitation playing in the background. Women in black attire and white shawls half covering their heads – my sisters and sisters-in-law, friends and family – will watch over her, cry quietly and, every now and then, raise a cacophony of wailing and weeping.

She will then be carried to the hearse once again and driven to the cemetery, on top of a hill nearby, not far from where my father, the newlywed groom, rented a small house and moved in with her. When she finally met her father-in-law, about two months later, they developed a fondness for each other that never waned – in her telling, the first hopeful sign in the long process of adaptation to her traumatic dislocation.

She will not, pointedly, be buried in her own ancestral village of Sh'hoor. And perhaps just as well as this would falsely trace a full circle. Despite the many instances of joy, pleasure and fulfilment in her long life, hers remained, for the most, a no-return departure – a trace of nostalgia for the other lives she could have had lingering in her, right until the last time I spoke to her.

# Rhm

The word for 'mercy' in Arabic is *rahma*, from the root *rahm*, for 'womb'. The two most commonly cited of the ninety-nine names of God are *rahman* and *raheem*, commonly translated as 'most compassionate' and 'most merciful', sometimes 'most gracious'.

The Prophet Mohammad is reported to have said: 'God says, glorified and sublime be He, I am the *rahman* and I have created the *rahm*, and I have drawn a name for her from mine, so that those who stayed bound to her, I am bound to them, and those who break with her, I banish.'

What is this bond that God speaks of, and how does one keep it once the umbilical cord is severed at one's birth? Will God turn his face away from me, now that my mother is no longer? Or did He already do so a long time ago?

# A Prayer

One of my oldest memories of my mother comes from those nights when she, Zakyeh, would be lounging with her sisters, Jameeleh and Safyeh, in their nightgowns in her bedroom. Her two siblings, who had settled in Tyre with their respective families, would have come to stay for a night or two at our house in Beirut, usually when my father was away. Of the three, my mother was the one who was deemed to have a 'good' voice and sometimes sang *ataba* to her sisters – ancient dirges with lyrics speaking of loss, separation and homesickness:

> *ya-hadya'l eess, sallemli ala immee*
> *w hkeelha alli jaraa lee*
> *w shkeelha hammee*

> *O red-roan rider, I pray you greet my mother,*
> *and tell her what has become of me,*
> *and share with her my woes*

But before their tears had had the time to dry, they would take to gossiping, teasing, even taunting each other a little, then quickly succumb to infectious laughter.

'Where did you buy this dress, sister? The butcher shop?'

'That woman walks like an armoured tank.'

'Let's face it, sister, your smile, all gums and no teeth, is not your best feature.'

The switch in the mood and the intensity of the women's merriment was uncanny, and a little frightening to me, as a child. Though I have far more childhood memories of my own three older sisters – and more vivid ones too – I do not recall anything of a similar nature between them.

Even more mysterious to me is the nebulous pleasure that my reminiscence of those nights gives me today. Perhaps, I tell myself, the three adult sisters were reverting, briefly and harmlessly, to a carefree childhood. After all, each had been married off at an early age, without much say in the matter; each had been fully claimed by motherhood and its hard labour; and each had her share of long-running domestic woes.

But there was something raucous about their complicity on those nights, some defiance in their capacity for joy, and a radiance to their mischief, including the little cruelties they aimed at each other. The ideals of decorum, piety and obedience that their social world held them to – coded in ancient scriptures and articulated in modern patriarchal norms – also demanded moderation and stoicism, and frowned upon any perceived excess of expression, whether in joy, anger or even mourning. Each of the three sisters would engage with such demands in her own way, every day, throughout their lives, sometimes complying, often negotiating and resisting, almost always converting the strictures into something they could live with.

Perhaps behind the flippancy and light-heartedness, the sisters were preserving an essence in themselves. Weavers whose fabric of choice was hope, they were hard at work, at night as in daytime, carving out viable lives, ones in which they loved and were loved aplenty. If so, no wonder that I, an accidental witness to their private revelries, prepubescent, safe as yet from the distorting strictures of masculinity, still draw, half a century later, some pleasure from the memory.

# Dark Tides

Slaughter breaks out in Israel and Palestine on 7 October 2023. Civilians bear the brunt as militants from Hamas and other Palestinian groups go on a rampage in southern Israel, shooting indiscriminately at young men and women at a music festival, occupying military bases, attacking and setting fire to settlements, and massacring whole families. They take more than two hundred people as hostages, including soldiers, women, children and the elderly, and drive them to Gaza, in the hope of exchanging them with Palestinian prisoners in Israeli jails.

Israel retaliates with indiscriminate bombing and collective punishment, depriving Gaza's more than two million people of water, electricity, food and medical supplies. Thousands of children are murdered by bombs falling from the sky. Their surviving peers, traumatised, will no doubt add to the foot soldiers of Palestinian resistance in ten or fifteen years from now – just as some of the militants who committed the latest atrocities may have witnessed carnage wrought by Israeli repression a decade or two ago when they themselves were children – a basic truth that the Israeli state seems incapable of understanding despite decades of empirical evidence.

Neither side is hiding its intention of targeting civilians, though only Israel finds its blinkered, ahistorical narrative of the conflict magnified in an echo chamber of friends and allies. The US and a handful of like-minded European states refuse to call for a ceasefire despite the genocidal carnage inflicted by the Israeli war machine on the population of Gaza. A language from colonial times re-erupts – 'barbarism and civilisation', 'evil', 'human animals', 'wiping out Hamas'. Joseph Conrad's 'exterminate the brutes' is very much in the air, as mainstream Western politicians line up in Tel Aviv to hug Benjamin Netanyahu and give Israel their unconditional support. For their part, Arab dictators, including the recently rehabilitated Bashar al-Assad, meet in Riyadh, wax lyrical about human rights and call for a ceasefire, for once reflecting the mood of their populations. They rightly accuse the West of double standards, but conveniently overlook their own records.

Meanwhile, in the first six weeks of the conflict alone, more than 12,000 Gazans – one in two hundred of the total population – are killed, including 5,000 children, and close to half of the population of 2.2 million is displaced. With a much stricter embargo in place since 7 October, the health system in tatters and over sixty percent of houses destroyed or damaged, Gaza has become unliveable. Over 100 hostages are exchanged for 240 detainees in Israeli jails. But many Palestinians remain behind bars while the fate of around 120 hostages remains uncertain. Several hostages have died in captivity, including some who may have been killed by Israeli bombardments of Gaza and during rescue attempts.

Germany and France ban pro-Palestinian demonstrations. Pro-Palestinian voices are cancelled, while many lose their jobs for taking a position against the carnage. Students at American universities are doxed. Accusations of antisemitism are dished out, while very real rises in antisemitic and Islamophobic incidents are recorded. Something dark is coming out of Europe and the US, and not just the Middle East.

Hope, a form of faith in the future, is in short supply.

# Faith

The Arabic words for 'faith', *eemaan*, and 'safety', *amaan*, have the same root, *amn*. Not so surprising, since the promise of inner peace has always been a draw card of religion. The word 'amen' also comes from the Hebrew *amn*, which reached old English via Latin and Greek. Several dictionaries give the meaning as 'truly' and 'verily' but also 'so be it'. It is an assertion of divine truth but there is a hint of resignation, of surrendering to God and whatever He has decreed. So does the word 'Islam', although the element of surrender here is much more explicit since to become a Muslim is, quite literally, to surrender to God and come to peace with oneself and the world. The Arabic word for 'surrender', *istislaam*, comes from the root word *silm*, 'peace'.

# Once Upon a Time

It is mid-autumn, just past midday, and still unseasonably hot. I am travelling from Beirut to Zahle, in the Beqaa Valley, an hour or so away, on the road to Damascus. It's an eastward journey away from the coastline, through steep roads, snaking up Mount Lebanon. Every now then, the Mediterranean shimmers into view through the gaps between buildings, both sad and reassuring, like a former home that can no longer hide its fragility from its children.

My driver is a chatty thirty-something man, but I am still a little jet-lagged and not in the mood for small talk. We are having a one-sided conversation about 'the situation' in the Arab world and the dire state of the Lebanese economy. He treats me to an inventory of all the problems the country is facing – the falling lira and soaring cost of living; how difficult it is to make ends meet, let alone marry and start a family; the number of beggars on the street, 'not just Syrians anymore, even Lebanese, would you believe it, who have never begged before'; how hopeless and corrupt our politicians are, how difficult it is to dislodge them, how we are heading to a catastrophe that only God can prevent . . .

The emotion in his voice has risen a little with every new item on the list. At least, I tell myself, this is a monologue to which I do not have to contribute; and all I have to do is sit tight until the storm has passed.

But then, unexpectedly, he looks at me in the rear-view mirror: 'What do you think will happen, *ya istez*?'

*Istez* is an honorific that means all of mister, sir and professor.

'*Ma hadaa b'yarif,*' I say flatly – 'Nobody knows' – determined not to add fuel to the conversation.

'*Shee bikaffir, ya zalami*' – 'Man, (this is enough to) make you lose your faith (in God)' – he replies, taking his eyes off me, giving up on his recalcitrant passenger. I have been demoted from *istez* to *zalami*, but at the least the pressure is off.

Shortly after, we stop in Shtoora. I wait in the taxi while my driver disappears into a shop to buy *areeshe w assal*, the cream cheese and honey the town is famous for, and I relish the silence I have been craving. The air outside my window is hot and humid; the seats are hard as wood. The trees lining the road are sun-stunned, their leaves drooping, the vivid green of their shoots long gone. The road reeks of molten rubber, memories of its potholes still fresh in my bones.

I try to doze off, but my mind is too alert. I find myself playing with the detritus of words that the gods of this land, long dead and gone, have left behind – *eeman* and *amaan*, *silm* and *istislaam*.

I, unconverted, unenchanted, savour nonetheless those words and contemplate the sweet, all-too-secular pleasure of giving up, of letting fate have its way with one's body, as it had done with God's. Of allowing myself to bid farewell, at long last, to the unloved century that has made my world. To give in, almost, to the ancient waves laying claim to me, like I almost did, once upon a time, a long time ago.

My driver returns, starts the engine and drives off, wordlessly. My mind's eye settles on the faded colours of summer, now streaming past me. I search in myself for hope, but the quest requires discipline, and the banishment of distractions, not least the interrogations to which my mind likes to treat me every now and then.

What is hope, where does it come from and what is it made of? Is it a gift of individual temperament, an emotional state, or an intrinsic feature of reality out there that one must learn how to find and nurture? Is it a force for good, a self-fulfilling, self-actualising form of energy, or a feat of human make-believe, almost always bound to be cruelly disappointing?

'Abandon all hope, all ye who enter here': what does the injunction, in Dante's *Inferno*, amount to? Is hopelessness a sine qua non, or even the very substance, of hell; or is it just a symptom of it, one of many, and not by far the worst? The Bible insists that 'hope maketh not ashamed'. But why should hope be associated with shame in the first place, so as to require rebuttal? Is it because despair is safer, more hard-headed, its bleakness more likely to be borne out by the world? Is there shame, then, in being wrong about the future? Or is hope a kind of false promise, an infectious one, and there is shame in leading others on, regardless of one's sincerity and good intentions?

'It takes schooled hope', Ernst Bloch wrote, but how does one *learn* hope?

I close my eyes, take a deep breath, banish the questions from my mind and focus on the most serene of thoughts I can conjure, helped no doubt by my low energy levels. Faces of loved ones, near and far, stream through my mind. My boys, Ann, my siblings, my friends in my new Australian home, my nieces and nephews born in Lebanon and spread around the world – uprooted yet prospering – and, not least, my Levantine friends, from Aleppo in the North to Ramallah in the South, from Baghdad in the East to Beirut's battered yet unbowed headland in the West: those who have stayed, and those who have left carrying with them small pieces of all-the-good-things-we-once-were, and spreading them in the world like charms or seeds, or just hanging them on the walls of their lives like good-fortune amulets.

The closing two sentences of Albert Camus's *Le mythe de Sisyphe* come back to me:

> *La lutte elle-même vers les sommets suffit à remplir un cœur d'homme. Il faut imaginer Sisyphe heureux.*

> The struggle itself toward the heights is enough to fill a man's heart. One must imagine Sisyphus happy.

Is this what keeps us going, the day-to-day quests and the small joys of kith and kin, despite the big calamities bearing down on us? There is something insistent, even urgent, in Camus' call – one *must* imagine – as if our lives depend on it.

Hope emerges in me like the peeling away of doubt, a one-sided cessation of hostilities, a rising-above rather than a surrender, a form of faith in something visceral but whose substance I cannot quite pinpoint. A kind of happy resignation – more stoicism of the aged perhaps, than optimism of the will.

There is hope in this shrug of an expression – *ma hada b'yarif* – a back-and-forth movement that releases the speaker from the immiserating urge to predict and shape one's destiny, loosening a little the future's grip on the present, while giving a grateful nod to the open-endedness of both.

I find a trace of hope too in that agnostic freethinker, and most pessimistic of Arab poets, Abu'l Alaa'l Maarri, author of *Risaalat al-Ghufran* – The Epistles of Forgiveness – who once lived not far from here. This is the man whose bust ISIS men saw fit to decapitate when they overran his native town of Maarra in Syria in 2013, almost a thousand years after his death.

Two verses of his now come back to me, like an incantation from a barely conceivable depth of time:

لَيسَت لَياليهِ مُحِسَّةُ كائِن
وُصِفَت بِسُرعَتِها وَلا إِبطائِها

Which, in Reynold Alleyne Nicholson's extraordinary translation, become:

*The Nights pass so,*
*Voices dumb,*
*Without sense quick or slow*
*Of what shall come*

# Epilogue

There is a long tradition of autobiographical writing in Arabic literature that goes back at least eight hundred years. The words for 'autobiography' in classical Arabic are *tarjamatu nafs*, which mean, literally, 'self-interpretation' or 'self-translation'. But the designation occurs most commonly as a verb, rather than a noun. One says, *X tarjama nafsahu*, 'X interpreted himself', which means 'X wrote an autobiography'.

This double emphasis – on interpretation, rather than depiction or representation, and on the act of writing, rather than its outcome – is more fertile than the flat 'autobiography'. 'Translation' implies transformation of some kind – one translates something into something else, and the English and French words 'translation' double up as a mathematical term meaning 'movement from one place to another', as opposed to 'rotation,' which is a change of orientation without displacement.

The word 'interpretation' points to the gap between the object of study – the self – and what is made of it through writing. It hints at the multiplicity of selves that could conceivably emerge from the exercise, depending on the various interpretive pathways open to the writer, some of which may be mutually exclusive. (I should know, having written two distinct memoirs based on the material of a single, somewhat eventful life.) In this sense, writing oneself becomes an open-ended gambit, rather than a simple exercise in recording one's life in words.

'Self-interpretation' also raises the question of the relation-ship, and the back-and-forth movement, between self and world, and the possibility that autobiographies are ways of bringing the world to bear upon the self, and vice versa. That is, the possibility that autobiographies are ways of interpreting the world through the prism of a single self, oneself, by teasing out or, conversely, seeking to obscure, the larger forces that have shaped one's subjectivity. Or, a little more naively, by formally using one's own life experience as the material evidence, the testing ground, for one's ideas about the world.

How the self emerges through autobiographical writing has been a point of contention among essayists in the Western tradition, from Montaigne onwards. What is the 'I' made of? Does its essence lie, as Merve Emre asks in her historical survey of the personal essay, in the drama of a chain of events, a writing style, the material demands of the publishing industry, the pre-constituted limitations on subjectivity imparted by bourgeois capitalism, or something else altogether? Is there something inherently misleading in conceiving of the self as sitting outside, and apart from, the world? The porous boundaries between self and world, and their mutually constitutive nature, remain at the heart of aesthetic and philosophical questions raised by autobiographical writing of all kinds.

But self-interpretation also hints at a closed-off, self-referential, even claustrophobic quality to autobiographies. After all, a woman writing her own life is not so unlike a writer reviewing her own work, a notion most people would find absurd. In other words, self-interpretation raises the prospect of self-as-prison or self-as-blinkers, limiting one's field of vision and one's ideas about the world. Every autobiography is also a tacit statement of limitations, a melancholy nod towards the larger, richer selves one has nipped in the bud, hardly noticing, because living is also an act of perpetual suppression, of shutting out and shutting down. All the conceptions, worldviews and other-ways-of-seeing, all the better places that we have been too close-minded or too predetermined – either way, too ungenerous, too wound up with our petty miseries and small comforts – to engage with.

That is to say, the abiding shadow of every autobiography is the hazy sketch of what one has failed to become – much like the history of the would-be-nations that are my homeland.

# Author's Note

The quotes in the epigraph come from page 35 of Muhyieddeen Ibn Arabi's collection of poems *The Translator of Desires*, translated by Michael Sells (Volume 147 in the Lockert Library of Poetry in Translation, Princeton University Press) and page 17 of Robin Robertson's *The Long Take* (Picador Poetry, 2018).

References to the essay as 'luck and play' and as 'digression', on the opening page, come from Theodor Adorno (page 93 of *The Adorno Reader*, edited by Brian O'Connor, Blackwell Publishing, 2000) and Walter Benjamin (page 28 of *The Origin of German Tragic Drama*, translated by John Osborne, Verso, 2006). Adorno wrote: 'Luck and play are essential to the essay. It does not begin with Adam and Eve but with what it wants to discuss; it says what is at issue and stops where it feels itself complete – not where there is nothing left to say.' Benjamin offered: 'Representation as digression – such is the methodological nature of the treatise. The absence of an uninterrupted purposeful structure is its primary characteristic. Tirelessly the process of thinking makes new beginnings, returning in a roundabout way to its original object.'

The first four paragraphs of the chapter 'I Dream of Jeannie' are a modified version of an excerpt from my own article 'Words, Swords and Insomniac Beauties', *Meanjin*, 2, 1999, pages 77-87.

In the chapter 'Lexicon of Love', I have drawn on Malek Chebel and Lassaâd Metoui's *Les cent noms de l'amour* (éditions Alternatives, première édition, Février, 2001), while the note about the word *shawq* comes from page xv of Michael Sells' introduction to his translation of Muhyiddeen Ibn Arabi's *The Translator of Desire*, referred to earlier. The Quranic excerpts in the chapter 'The God Years' are suraat 81 (*al-Takweer*) and 89 (*al-Fajr*), translation by N. J. Dawod's *The Koran* (Penguin Books, 1974). In the same chapter, the figure of 7,000 books in Kitabu'l Fahrast is based on Shawkat M Toorawa's 'Proximity, Resemblance, Sidebars and Clusters: Ibn al-Nadeem's Organizational Principles in Fihrist 3.3', *Oriens*, 2010, 38, 217–247); the quote estimating that 100 books out of those 7,000 are about love is taken from page 17 of Chebel and Metoui, cited above.

Much has been written, in Lebanon and Israel, about the Verdun operation described in the chapter 'Bullet, Paper, Rock'. Recent writing by Israeli investigative journalist Ronen Bergman casts doubt on several aspects of the official Israeli narrative and its mythologised version in the Steven Spielberg 2005 movie *Munich*. Ronen is a political and military analyst for the daily Yediot Ahronoth who has conducted extensive research on Israeli assassination policies, drawing on his access to the Israeli intelligence community. He asserts that the three Palestinian leaders killed in the operation had no connection to the Munich Olympics attack on Israeli athletes, and that the actual masterminds were not targeted in the operation (see David Horovitz interviewing Ronen Bergman, 'How Israel's leaders use targeted killings to try to "stop history"', *The Times of Israel*, 26 January 2018, https://www.timesofisrael.com/how-israels-leaders-use-targeted-killings-to-try-to-stop-history/ (accessed 8 December 2023) and Uri Mesgav's Why Israel 1973's Beirut Raid Was too Successful. *Haaretz*, 12 May 2023 https://www.haaretz.com/israel-news/2023-05-12/ty-article-magazine/.highlight/why-israels-1973-beirut-raid-was-too-successful/00000188-0caa-d4b7-a3f9-cfaaca790000 (accessed 8 December 2023).

The discussion on violence in the chapter 'Bullet, Paper, Rock' refers to page 51 of Frantz Fanon's *Wretched of the Earth* (translated by Richard Philcox, Grove Press, 2004), pages 4 and 52–56 of Hannah Arendt's *On Violence* (Harvest Books, 1970), and pages 44–47 of Walter Benjamin's *Towards the Critique of Violence: A Critical Edition* (edited by Peter Fenves and Julia Ng, Stanford University Press, 2021). In referring to Fanon's work, I use the word 'detoxify' instead of the more widely employed 'cleanse', as argued by Kathryn Batchelor, among others ('Fanon's Les Damnés de la Terre: Translation, De-Philosophization and the Intensification of Violence', *Nottingham French Studies*, 2015, 54.1, 7–22).

The quote in the chapter 'Conditional Fluency' comes from pages 62–63 of Pierre Bourdieu's *Ce que parler veut dire: l'économie des échanges linguistiques* (Language and Symbolic Power, translated by Gino Raymond and Matthew Adamson, Polity Press, 1982).

In the chapter 'Lingua Franca', I mention the dice numbers widely used by backgammon players in the Levant. In my memoir *Leave to Remain*, published in 2009, I wrote mistakenly that these numbers are of Turkish origin. I have since learnt that they are actually Persian. The 1001 Nights quote at the end of the chapter 'Letters of the Sun and Letters of the Moon' comes from page 25 of *The Arabian Nights*, translated by Husain Haddawy, based on the text of the fourteenth-century Syrian manuscript edited by Muhsin Mahdi (W. W. Norton, 1990).

In the chapter 'Can the Subaltern Run?' I am of course referring to Gayatri Chakravorty Spivak's famous 1988 essay 'Can the Subaltern Speak?' The reference to the 'rush of things' in the chapter 'Mukhayyar aw Mussayyar' is from Don DeLillo's *The Names* (Vintage Contemporaries, 1982). The translation of the table of contents of Ibn Hazm's *Ring of the Dove*, in the eponymous chapter, is my own.

The description of the Hiroshima bomb cloud in the chapter *Anatomy of Collapse* comes from pages 162–163 of Michihiko Hachiya's *Hiroshima Diary: The Journal of a Japanese Physician, August 6 – September 30, 1945* (edited by Warner Wells, University of North Carolina Press, 1955).

The Prophet's saying about the *rahm* and *rahman*, quoted in the chapter 'Rhm', is hadeeth 1694 in *Sinan Abu Daoud Assajastaani, Kitaab Azzakat*, which can be found at hadithprophet.com/hadith-1444.html (accessed on 18 November 2023). The translation of the saying from Arabic to English is my own.

In the chapter 'Dark Tides', I took the figures of 12,000 Gazans killed, including 5,000 children, from Reuters ('Gazans Flee Key Southern City', https://www.reuters.com/world/middle-east/israel-renews-call-gazans-flee-key-southern-city-2023-11-17/, accessed on 19 November 2023), over a million displaced from the *New York Times* ('Gaza Palestinians Displaced', https://www.nytimes.com/2023/10/14/world/middleeast/gaza-palestinians-displaced.html, accessed on 19 November 2023) and over 60% of houses destroyed or damaged from the UN Secretary General António Guterres reported in the Guardian (Israel-Gaza war blog, https://www.theguardian.com/world/live/2023/dec/09/israel-gaza-war-live-us-criticised-for-veto-on-un-resolution-calling-for-ceasefire-with-hamas?page=with:block-6574ed858f0848ff947d5b23&filterKeyEvents=false#liveblog-navigation, accessed on 12 December 2023).

The quote in the chapter 'Once Upon a Time' comes from page 166 of Albert Camus' *Le mythe de Sisyphe – Essai sur l'absurde*, Gallimard, Collection Idées, 1942; the English translation of the quote is from The *Myth of Sisyphus and Other Essays*, translated from the French by Justin O'Brien, Vintage Books, 1955. Abu al-Alaa al-Maari's verses in the

same chapter are taken from the poem السَّاع آنية الحوادث ما حوت ,
which can be found at aldiwan.net/poem22033.html (accessed
on 18 November 2023). The translation of these verses, given
in the same chapter, are by Reynold Alleyne Nicholson, taken
from poem 77 on page 103 of his *Translations of Eastern Poetry
and Prose*, Cambridge University Press, 1922.

Reading *Interpreting the Self: Autobiography in the Arabic
Literary Tradition*, edited by Dwight F. Reynolds (University
of California Press, 2001) has been an eye-opener for me and
one of the inspirations for the Epilogue. Also in the Epilogue, I
refer to Merve Emre's essay 'The Illusion of the First Person',
published in the *New York Review of Books* of 3 November
2022. I am aware that I have only paraphrased the question
Emre asks in her essay, as well as some of the answers, and
paraphrasing can be a dangerous business. I hope that in this I
have not done any violence to her work – or, for that matter, to
any of the works I cite above.

# A Note on Transliteration of Arabic Words into English

In transliterating Arabic words into English, I sought to maintain a balance between simplicity and phonetic accuracy. Where words have a widely encountered English form and spelling (e.g. Tyre, Leila, Beirut), I used those. Otherwise, I wrote a transliteration that is as phonetically close to the Arabic original as possible without resorting to special characters that require some expertise on the part of the reader.

For example, to reproduce the long a in Arabic, I used 'aa', rather than the 'ā' adopted by some academic transliteration systems. The letters 'q' and 'k' stood for the strong and weak 'k' of Arabic, respectively. Hence, I used Laathiqiya rather than the Anglicised version Latikia, and Shahrazaad and Shahrayaar instead of Sheherazade and Shehryar.

On the other hand, for simplicity's sake, I did not use any extra characters or diacritic signs to convey Arabic letters with no English equivalent, and resorted instead to the nearest-sounding English letters, at the expense of phonetic accuracy (e.g. ع and ح were written as a and h, respectively); the only exception to the use of diacritic signs occurred in the chapter 'Letters of the Sun and Letters of the Moon' for reasons that are quite obvious from the context.

# Photo Credits

Page 25 in chapter *I Dream of Jeannie*: A scene from sitcom I Dream of Jeannie: Michael Ansara, (as the Blue Djinn), Barbara Eden, Larry Hagman, in Season 2 episode 'Happy Anniversary' (Everett Collection Inc / Alamy Stock Photo).

Page 29 in chapter *Lexicon of Love*: Cover page of manuscript of Kitabu'l fahrast by Ibn al-Nadeem (CBL Ar 3315, f.1r, © The Trustees of the Chester Beatty Library, Dublin).

Page 35 in chapter *An Honourable Woman*: My mother, right, aged 40, with my father's cousin Naziha and my youngest brother Hekmat (circa 1974) (photo from family album).

Page 43 in chapter *Homemaking*: My father, my younger brother Hekmat (front) and myself (photo from family album).

Page 57 in chapter *Bullet, Paper, Rock*: Manara lighthouse in Beirut (photo by author).

Page 66 in chapter The Karate Years: Fury of the Dragon, US, poster, Bruce Lee, 1976 (Everett Collection Inc / Alamy Stock Photo).

Page 83 in chapter *Tribes in Trouble*: My end-of-year class picture in *classe huitième* (year 5, primary school) with our cruel teacher Monsieur Berbéri; I am in the back row, 3rd from the left (photo from family album).

Page 87 in chapter *Tribes in Trouble*: Our much-loved French literature teacher Monsieur Soulier (photo from family album).

Page 93 in chapter *The War is Over*: La Guerre est Finie (aka THE WAR IS OVER), top from left: Yves Montand, Ingrid Thulin, Yves Montand (centre), bottom from left Yves Montand, Genevieve Bujold (Everett Collection Inc / Alamy Stock Photo).

Page 97 in chapter *Sifr*: Photo of excerpt from an al-Khawarizmi manuscript (The Bodleian Libraries, University of Oxford, Bodleian Library MS. Huntington 214, fol. 4b-5a, image 1).

Page 102 in chapter *Empire Strikes Back*: Opening page of first volume of Antoine Galland's translation of the 1001 Nights.

Page 110 in chapter *Lingua Franca*: Extract from Kamal al-Din al-Hasan ibn 'Ali ibn al-Hasan al-Farisi, 'The Book of Correction of Optics for those who have Sight and Mind', partly based on Ibn al-Haytham's work, Persia, probably Tabriz, dated 708 AH/1309 AD, Sotheby. (Manuscripts and Archives Division, The New York Public Library. "Tanqîh al-manâzir ... New York Public Library Digital Collections).

Page 115 in chapter *Letters of the Sun and Letters of the Moon*: A page from the 10th night of the 1001 Nights, Arabic Bulaq version, 1826.

Page 125 in chapter *West Hall*: Photo of West Hall at the American University of Beirut (permission granted from American University of Beirut Media Office, copyrights American University of Beirut).

Page 155 in chapter *The Lucky Country*: the Bay Run in Sydney's inner West at dusk (photo by author).

Page 159 in chapter *Ring of the Dove*: Photo of opening page of manuscript of Ring of the Dove by Ibn Hazm al-Andalusi; Opening05 (incl. f001a) from Tawqal hamama fil ulfa wal ullif, Leiden University Digital Collections (Creative Commons CC BY License).

Page 167 in chapter *The September Years*: Photo of the Falling Man, New York, Twin Towers, September 11, 2001 (Jose Jimenez/ Primera Hora/ Getty Images News via Getty Images).

Page 172 in chapter Gifts of Return: Campus of the American University of Beirut (photo by Ahmad El Itani, permission granted from American University of Beirut Media Office, copyrights American University of Beirut).

Page 190 in chapter *A Self-Insight*: My father with his uncle Jaafar (right) and his cousin Abu Mustafa (left). (Photo from family album).

Page 208 in chapter *Lotteries of the Mind*: My mother (right) with her brother Abdel Ameer and his wife Effat, shortly after their marriage (early 1970s). (Photo from family album).

Page 212 in chapter *Untouched*: The Eastern Mediterranean. (Photo by author).

# Acknowledgements

I owe much to many. My agent Jane Novak is a force of nature whose belief in the book is the kind of blessing that every writer wishes for. Terri-ann White has been a joy to work with, from the first time we met right through many conversations over the following months. I am grateful to David Winter for his thorough reading of the manuscript and excellent suggestions. Thank you to Becky Chilcott and Keith Feltham.

My conversations with my friend Ghassan Hage, especially our weekday lunches in Sydney, have been a stimulating delight. It was on one of those occasions that Ghassan pointed me to Pierre Bourdieu's *Ce que parler veut dire* when I mentioned to him that I was writing about my experience of multilingualism in Beirut. Thank you to Hiam and Hekmat El-Zein who read excerpts of the manuscript and were generous with feedback, not to mention warmth, laughter and, when we're in the same city, hospitality like no other. Thank you to Caroline Alcorso for her friendship and conviviality over several weekends in Currarong, during one of which I made big strides in the writing of this book. Thank you to Jihad El-Zein for sharing his understanding of Middle Eastern politics and to Terry Petry for many long walks and thoughtful questions. Thank you to Kanny Hannah for her brilliant insights and sense of humour.

Thank you to Iman, Helen, Samer, Livia, Fadi, Huda, Bassel, and, not least, my tribe of five siblings, four in-laws, and thirteen nephews and nieces with their seven partners (seven in total, not each) – rooted exiles and homemaking nomads with whom I have experienced the joys, tragedies and small pleasures of Lebanon and the Arab world over many years.

Love and gratitude to my wife Ann, always my first and most generous reader, and my boys Ali and Sami. Critics at large, partners in crime and absolute rockstars: to them I owe the most.

**About Upswell**

Upswell Publishing was established in
2021 by Terri-ann White as a not-for-profit
press. A perceived gap in the market for
distinctive literary works in fiction, poetry
and narrative non-fiction was the motivation.
In her years as a bookseller, writer and then
publisher, Terri-ann has maintained a watch
on literary books and the way they insinuate
themselves into a cultural space and are
then located within our literary and cultural
inheritance. She is interested in making books
to last: books with the potential to still be
noticed, and noted, after decades and thus
be ripe to influence new literary histories.

**About this typeface**

Book designer Becky Chilcott chose
Foundry Origin not only as a strong,
carefully considered, and dependable
typeface, but also to honour her late
friend and mentor, type designer Freda
Sack, who oversaw the project. Designed
by Freda's long-standing colleague,
Stuart de Rozario, much like Upswell
Publishing, Foundry Origin was created
out of the desire to say something new.